Golf in the High Zone

The mind game finally explained

Golf in the High Zone

'The mind game finally explained'

Published by
HVT Publishing
3 Durham Road, Wolviston, TS22 5LP, England

Author Steve Wharton

ISBN: 9781549893797

A CIP record is available for this book from the British Library

Published in Great Britain by HVT Publishing

Contents

'The mind game finally explained'

'The mind game finally explained'

Foreword

Have you ever wondered why you have played your best golf on special occasions such as your birthday, anniversary, father's day/mothers day or even after a special event such as getting married, birth of a child etc? This doesn't just happen to you, it happens to the best golfers in the world. I didn't really know why this happened to me until I met Steve. I now know and so will you after reading this book.

After meeting Steve I became aware of high vibrational thinking and this enabled me to understand why I played my best golf when I was at my happiest. And with this knowledge I could learn to control my thinking and not simply wait to be happy to play well. I was able to use high vibrational thinking to encourage a state of mind that was filled with happiness and love therefore increasing the chances of peak performance.

Most of the techniques which Steve explains in this book are not overly complex and are often common sense. I believe the people who will gain the most from discovering these techniques are the people who will have the commitment to change their thinking. I had been made aware of more sports psychology techniques probably than most people due to my background as a player and coach, but I wasn't really using the information correctly – Steve's simple explanation of how it all actually works really helped me understand how to use it.

As a player, being in the zone doesn't come around very often. It is that day when every putt goes in, every drive sails down the fairway, and most golfers have had at least one of these days. Steve's book can help you understand why the zone happens and how you can intentionally put yourself into the zone.

If there is one thing I have learnt from my time as a golfer and coach it is that players become what they think of themselves. If you think of yourself as a 28 handicapper that is what you will always be. If you think of yourself as a club champion and truly believe it, I have no doubt you will achieve it. Your thinking is a choice and your mood is a choice. Everything around you can affect your thinking, your mood, your vibration. Once you have learnt to spot this then you can learn to control it and learn to make this choice. Choosing your mood and your thinking sounds very easy, but it is one of the hardest things to do and stick to.

There is so much negativity in the world, in people, in the media etc it is extremely difficult to be positive and remain positive. I initially changed my thinking on the golf course, I then expanded this to my practice routine and then to the journey to the course. I now use these techniques in everyday life, at home and with my children.

My favourite technique was one of the first things Steve ever taught me and it was a simple task to highlight all of the negativity that was keeping me out of the high zone. My task was to carry a notebook and write down all of the negative thoughts that came into my head. After the first few hours I was filling pages and pages of this small notebook. This really highlighted to me how everything around me, including people and activities were affecting my thinking and ultimately my golf performances. The next step was to cut down the amount of negative thoughts I had which was a lot easier when I became aware of them.

Using this technique on the golf course highlighted to me on certain holes/shots I didn't have any negative thoughts and on others I had more than I ever thought possible. My advice to you is to embrace the ideas in this book and be committed to improving your thinking. It is a choice and probably the most important choice you make.

The techniques recommended by Steve can have a massive effect not just on your golf performance but your everyday life.

Simon Robinson BSc PGCE
PGA Golf Instructor Sharpley Golf Academy

Introduction

This book contains information that will transform your ability to play golf, after reading it you will have a new empowering understanding of how your mind works and how this relates to peak performance on the golf course.

This knowledge will enable you to attain the magical 'zone' or step into a state of 'flow' at will. Yes it will take a little practice but not that much, certainly not the amount of effort it took to learn to swing a golf club correctly. Before you know it you will be playing golf on another level altogether.

The key to this is having a clear understanding of exactly what the 'zone' is, how you get there and why you can play so well when you are there, questions that I believe have never yet been answered, until now that is.

Just to be clear the 'zone' is what sports psychologists call it when you are performing at your very peak, that magical day when everything seems to go your way. It is oft described as:

'Being in the flow in a state of spontaneous joy and super productivity and it usually only occurs in short bursts'.

The reason I can give you the answers to these key questions is thanks to an amazing concept called 'High Vibrational Thinking', which effectively breaks everything down to the sub-atomic level, the energy level. This enables a simple and clarified viewpoint to be obtained, which empowers you with a new perspective shifting your thinking in the process. And this is the key to understanding and being able to attain the 'zone' at will. From this point forward I will refer to it as the **'High Zone'** as I feel this more aptly describes where you actually are, all will soon become clear.

I have also included various methods which I have called modules and you can use these modules to train yourself to move closer to and into the 'high zone' at will. The modules are to be used in the best way that suits you; a module that one person prefers may not be the module of choice of another person or vice versa. Or you may like to use two or three modules at any one time. Whatever your preference there will be a number of modules that you can adapt into your routine.

'Golf in the High Zone' will not only help change the way that you think but also the way that you feel on the golf course and this is what will empower you to be able to manoeuvre yourself into or close to the high zone, which will enable you to play golf more consistently at your very best. You will up your mental game 100% when you understand exactly how it works and become proficient at using one or more of the techniques provided. This is what makes the difference between average golfers and outstanding golfers the ability to embody the correct mindset.

Talent, determination and relentless practice can only get you so far, you must also be able to use your mind to be able to push back the boundaries of what is possible. Sports psychologists have looked at this closely over the years and come up with many good ideas and methods to help to try and get you there but there was always one thing missing.

They were never really able to explain what the elusive zone ('high zone') was or why when you attain it you can play so well. How was it that you seemed to get the luck of the bounce and everything went your way? What was going on to make this happen? Why did good fortune smile on you? Why did the magic happen? Why were the golfing gods with you? And why was it usually so fleeting and short lived?

Without knowing exactly what it was and how it worked was always going to make it very difficult if not impossible to intentionally put yourself in the 'high zone', and on the rare occasion when you did find yourself somehow miraculously there it could and did slip away at any time. Through this book you are about to find out exactly what the 'high zone' is and why you can play better when you are there and also how you can put yourself there when you need to. And also what holds you back from this magical place the majority of the time and what you can do to change that so you naturally exist closer to it or even in it more often.

This priceless knowledge is the key to you being able to more consistently attain and hold yourself in this amazing place where you can play golf way beyond your 'normal' level. Knowing what it is, why it works and how to get there brings the missing pieces of the jigsaw to the table and this is what makes these ten modules so powerful.

Up until now the emphasis and focus has been on the physical (the mechanics of the swing) and technical side (the equipment) of golf but the time has come to blend mind, body and the technical which will enable golfers of the future to really push back the boundaries.

In fact this book applies to any sport not just golf because all performances move completely up to another level when you attain the high zone or move closer to it. Quite simply put these modules work in any theatre of sport or indeed life, but before I reveal to you the secrets first I must explain to you the concept of High Vibrational Thinking.

Chapter 1

High Vibrational Thinking

*"If you want to find the secrets of the Universe,
think in terms of energy, frequency and vibration"*

Dr Nikola Tesla 1942

Serbian-American inventor, electrical engineer, mechanical engineer,
physicist, and futurist

Dr Nikola Tesla is still regarded as one of the world's outstanding intellects; he paved the way for many of the technological developments of modern times. It's quite amazing to think that his words in 1942 could be so relevant today as we progress to a greater understanding of our world. His reference to energy, frequency and vibration could not be more apt as we explore the intricate workings of the Universe and unlock the real secrets of this amazing world of energy that we live in.

High Vibrational Thinking is understanding our world from the viewpoint of energy. The first step in achieving this is looking at everything as particles of energy. It's all made from atoms and beyond that subatomic particles. The car you drive, the house you live in, the clothes you wear, the food you eat, your family pet, your bed, your body, yes everything that you think is solid and made from matter, is in fact energy.

This also includes your thoughts, feelings and emotions. It's all energy and the trillions of different things we see in our world is this energy manifesting in different ways. What makes everything appear different and separate from us is caused by the different vibrational frequency that everything has.

Look at water, if you freeze it and slow down its vibration it turns into ice. If you heat it and speed up its vibration it turns into steam. It's still water just appearing in different forms depending on its vibration.

Like everything else we too are made from energy and our personal energy field vibrates at a frequency, which can vary in its vibrational rate depending on the thoughts and feelings that we harbour. You see thoughts and feelings are also energy and influence our lives much more than we may realise, just like radio waves they are there in the air all around us although we can't actually see them.

Our thoughts and feelings and to some degree even the thoughts and feelings of other people have a very real affect upon us. They affect us by raising or lowering the frequency of our personal energy field, depending on whether or not they are high vibrational or low vibrational in nature.

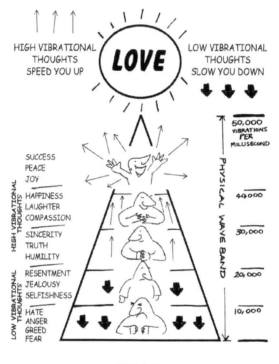

FEAR

(This diagram is for illustration purposes only and the estimation of vibrations per millisecond is not to be taken as fact.)

The sun represents love the fastest vibrating energy that we know and at the other end of the scale is fear the slowest vibrating energy. Our world exists within these two parameters and as we are also energy our personal energy vibration fluctuates between these two poles depending on our thoughts, feelings and emotions.

When we are full of laughter and joy we vibrate at the higher levels. When we are angry or upset this drags down our vibration and we vibrate at the lower levels. The pyramid represents our climb in life back to our natural state, which is love.

It's a world of energy that we live in and it's all vibrating. You could see the energy particles vibrating if you had a powerful enough microscope. Science tells us that the fastest vibrating energy in our world is love and the slowest vibrating energy is fear.

This ties in with the 'Emotional Guidance Scale' as explained by Esther and Jerry Hicks in 'Ask and it is Given' (Hay House Publications) The scale depicts the following emotions beginning with the most positive empowering emotions down to the negative emotions of desperation, weakness and fear.

*Love/knowledge/Empowerment/Freedom/

*Joy/Appreciation/Passion

* Enthusiasm/Eagerness/Happiness

* Positive expectation/Belief

* Optimism

* Hopefulness

* Contentment

* Boredom

* Pessimism

* Frustration/Irritation/Impatience

* Disappointment

* Doubt/Worry/Blame

* Discouragement

* Anger/Hatred/Rage

* Jealousy

* Insecurity/Guilt/unworthiness

* Fear/Grief/Depression/Despair/Powerlessness

As you can see the 'Ask and it is Given' scale is very similar to the scale depicted in the High Vibrational Thinking pyramid, low vibrational stuff at the bottom and high vibrational stuff at the top.

> *'Love is what we are born with. Fear is what we learn. The spiritual journey is the unlearning of fear and prejudices and the acceptance of love back in our hearts. Love is the essential reality and our purpose on earth. To be consciously aware of it, to experience love in ourselves and others, is the meaning of life. Meaning does not lie in things. Meaning lies in us'.*

-Marianne Williamson-
American spiritual teacher, author and lecturer

Eloquently put, the fear or negative energy that we take on board during our lives is what we must learn to get rid of. This will allow us to rise in vibration bringing love back into our lives. This is the spiritual journey, the unlearning of fear and rising up in vibration back into love. This is the purpose of life to rise up to the vibration of love and vibrate in harmony with it, to be love.

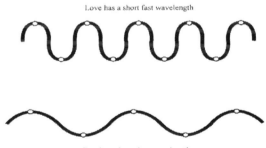

Love has a short fast wavelength

Fear has a long slow wavelength

Everybody has experienced the energy in different places or at different times. At Christmas we all feel the general rise in vibration, as the festive spirit takes hold. Problems and worries are put to one side and we switch off the negativity while we enjoy the Christmas period.

This is what you are feeling, the collective energy of everybody forgetting about their problems for a few days, which results in a rise in vibration virtually right across the world. And doesn't it feel good? This is what it could be like all of the time if we could stop the negative thoughts and feelings within every individual permanently.

Then January hits with the collective energy plunging into the negative zone, as everybody starts to worry about the extra money spent over Christmas and the debts they have run up. This is why January feels like it does and it is also why more people take sick days than at any other time of the year. It's a month when we collectively do more negative thinking and feeling than at any other time of the year.

I am sure that we all know, that when we are full of laughter and joy that this makes us feel good, what has actually happened is the high vibrational energy of joy and laughter has pulled up the frequency of our personal energy field. The same effect can be experienced when we achieve something such as passing our driving test, passing our exams, scoring a goal, winning a competition, receiving praise for a job well done, sinking a forty foot putt etc.

What happens is that we suddenly feel good about ourselves, we feel successful and happy and we have good high vibrational thoughts about ourselves, this pulls up the frequency of our personal energy field.

So as you can see high vibrational thoughts and feelings such as laughter, joy, honesty, sincerity, truth, compassion, etc keep our energy field vibrating at the higher levels making us feel good.

Whereas low vibrational thoughts and feelings such as anger, hate, jealousy, envy, greed, selfishness, etc slow down our energy field making us feel bad. This is why we use phrases such as 'I'm down in the dumps', 'I'm flat as a pancake', to describe when we feel bad and 'I'm high as a kite', 'I'm buzzing' to describe when we feel good we are really referring to the frequency of our personal energy field.

The faster our energy field vibrates the better we feel because the closer we are to the frequency of love; this is why we spend virtually all of our lives trying to make ourselves feel better. So it makes sense to try and keep our personal energy field vibrating at the higher levels, 'I mean do you want to feel down in the dumps?'

Learning to see and think about our world in terms of energy is the very basic fundamental principle of High Vibrational Thinking. Once you understand that everything in our world is energy, you can begin to see things in a new and very empowering way. This new perspective gives you far greater control, over everyday situations and events, which you previously may have thought were largely beyond your control.

HVT is becoming aware of your thinking and trying to consciously think high vibrational thoughts as much of the time as you can. The higher vibrational thoughts mean a better life; all of life's problems exist at the lower vibrational levels. This means your general or average vibrational frequency determines how smooth your life will run. So a very negative person who engages in lots of negative thinking will experience more problems and negative situations than a more positive thinking person.

I am sure everybody knows somebody whose life lurches from one problem to another, it's all to do with the way they think and feel. This does happen to us all but some people experience it much more severely.

A person that exists at the lower vibrational levels due to their excessive negative thinking will experience the types of energy that exist at those levels. Anger, frustration, worry, greed, envy, dishonesty, hate, jealousy, fear etc, will be normal everyday experiences. They will get more parking tickets, accidents, arguments, speeding fines, job dissatisfaction, bad service, poor health and even age a lot quicker.

In general they will experience more misfortune than somebody that consistently thinks in a more high vibrational way.

Another way of describing someone that has excessive negative thoughts and exists predominately in the lower vibrational zones is to say they have low self-esteem or low self-worth, it's the same thing. Obviously because they are down there they will feel worse about themselves. Raise their vibration and you will also raise their self-esteem and self-worth.

Of course we all experience the ups and downs of life and things go wrong but the higher your general vibration the better it will be. You see low vibrational things exist at low vibrational levels; you can't experience them if you are vibrating at the higher levels. Just like you can't be sad and depressed when you are happy the two cannot exist together.

The trick is to stay at the higher vibrational levels all of the time then you would have very few problems in your life. In fact you will find the more you focus on using HVT the more things will go your way, good things will happen to you more often.

You will experience more success, good fortune, happiness, peace, love, better health in fact everything improves. Your life right across the board will be better, less negative encounters, less conflict and you will find life runs a lot smoother for you.

In terms of golf the higher you are vibrating the better you will be able to play, it's as simple as that. This is why I call it the 'high zone' but there is one big problem that gets in the way and we all have it, inner resistance.

Chapter 2

Inner Resistance

*'Your task is not to seek for love, but merely to seek and find
all the barriers within yourself that you have built against it'.*

-Rumi-

13th-century Persian Sunni Muslim poet, jurist, Islamic scholar,
theologian, and Sufi mystic

Your 'inner resistance' is the negative emotional energy that you
have trapped inside of you and this 'inner resistance' is pulling
you down in vibration away from the fastest vibrational energy
that we know, love. Your inner resistance is the barrier within
yourself that is keeping you away from love.

Everybody has this and it is mainly created, in the first five or six
years of our lives. During this very sensitive time period we are
operating just like a computer and downloading data. Everything
that we experience and are taught we soak up like a sponge.

The main source of our early years information download is our
parents and close family. Our early experiences are accepted
without question, as we absorb whatever is going on around us.
We believe what we see and hear and from this information
downloading we begin forming our 'inner resistance' as some of
the negative energies that we encounter and experience gets
stuck in our energy field.

Every negative thought, feeling and emotion leaves its mark in
your energy field and this accumulation of dark sludge is your
inner resistance. The bad part is that the negative energy that
gets stuck is very difficult to shift because every time we feel it,
this recharges it and this keeps it strong within us. Energies like
anger, hate, fear, frustration, worry, stress, jealously and fear all
become part of our energy field and these slow vibrating energies
collectively drag us down in vibration. And this is all picked up
from everyday things we see and experience happening in front of
us.

At the age of around six-years old we more or less stop the
downloading and whatever we have downloaded up until that
point becomes well and truly entrenched. It's a bit like loading a
program onto a computer only this time it has been loaded into
our mind. And like a computer we are limited by the program, we

can only do what the program can do; some people call this living within our comfort zone.

Of course after six-years old our comfort zones may change slightly as the years go by but in general the downloading in place at six-years old stays more or less the same. This negative energy that everybody downloads is what I call your 'inner resistance' some people call it your inner demons or trapped emotions. And because it is heavy slow vibrational energy, it slows down your natural vibration and holds you down at a lower vibrational level. A level that you get used to and accept as where you belong, this is what I call our vibrational comfort zone.

A person that has experienced a very positive energy upbringing, which would be happy, loving caring parents, few family arguments, very little negative energy from the TV, DVD's and computer games may only have a small amount of 'inner resistance' holding them down so they would exist generally at quite a high vibrational level.

A person subject to a large amount of negative energy such as lots of family arguments, family money problems, maybe your parents split up when you were young, family feelings of frustration, bullying, stress, worry, greed, hatred, negative gossiping and fear could end up with a lot of negative energy stuck inside them, creating a powerful and heavy form of 'inner resistance'. So they would exist generally at a lower vibrational level.

This 'inner resistance' has a powerful influence over us and can sometimes distort and twist our mind so much that we behave in dysfunctional ways, I think we have all done that at sometime in our lives. 'Inner resistance' is the major factor in all negative behaviour. Bullying, anti-social behaviour, crime, violence, vandalism, self-harming, alcoholism, drug addiction, gang culture, lack of respect, selfishness, depression, etc are all negative manifestations that occur because of the inner resistance we carry.

Our 'inner resistance' is where all the negative feelings that we have about ourselves and the world around us are stored. It is where our unhappiness dwells within us, it is our unhappiness.

It is slow vibrating energy and when it contaminates our energy field it slows our energy vibration down and drags us further away from the vibration of love. The further away from love we are the worse it feels and the more likely we are to malfunction and encounter problems in our lives.

Maybe you feel your parents didn't show you as much love as you would have liked them to but remember they also have 'inner resistance' and they can't help lots of the things that they do or did, just like you sometimes. They are doing the best that they can under the influence of their 'inner resistance'. Maybe they let you down sometimes or don't spend much time with you or even don't tell you or have never told you that they love you. This just means that they have a strong 'inner resistance' controlling them and probably don't even realise they are doing these things. This is just them malfunctioning.

Many of us develop most of our inner resistance through our relationship with our parents. Lack of love in this department makes it fertile ground for negativity to take root. It gets established at an early impressionable age and forces us into repetitive patterns of negative thinking and feeling, which ensures its survival.

It's not our parents fault, they couldn't help it and continuing to blame them simply keeps you locked in the cycle of negative thinking, which in turn keeps feeding your inner resistance. They couldn't help whatever they may have done to make you feel 'unloved', you must release the negativity you feel around this subject. And you do that by understanding how it works (which you now do) and forgiving them because they really did not do it their inner resistance did, this frees you up from the bad feelings.

Let it go and you will rise in vibration. Hold on to the bad feelings and you will be trapped. Trapped by blame, hate, anger, resentment, frustration and bitterness etc. They were used and controlled by their inner resistance understand this and you will be free.

Your 'inner resistance' is like your mobile phone battery and needs to be charged up everyday only you don't plug it in and charge it up with electricity, it gets recharged by your negative thoughts and feelings. And it does this by getting you to feel bad. The worse you feel the more it gets charged up. It wants you to get angry, feel upset, be frustrated, feel jealous or feel depressed and unhappy. It is the little voice in your head encouraging you to feel bad.

It's like a little gremlin living inside you that wants negative bad things to happen so that you feel bad. This is how it survives. It is controlling you and encouraging you to see things in a negative way. It will talk you into believing anything that gets it what it wants; it is the thoughts in your head that are negative and it wants as much negativity from you as it can get.

It sparks into life many times during your day prompting you to react to things in a negative way. Maybe you lose your key and get **frustrated** and **angry** because you can't find it. Your negative reaction, your **frustration** and **anger** is what your 'inner resistance' wants. When you are looking for your key it is the little voice in your head saying things like 'you will be late', 'you will have to buy a new key', 'what if somebody has stolen it', etc. You just listen to the thoughts and get angry and frustrated. The little gremlin is winning; it is satisfying its need for negative energy.

This is how it stays strong within you, by topping up its battery everyday through your negative thoughts, feelings and emotions. You get angry and you recharge its battery, you worry, feel stressed, feel jealous, feel upset, feel depressed, feel irritated, feel envious, feel guilty, feel annoyed, feel unloved or feel disillusioned, you are topping up its battery.

So the more powerful your 'inner resistance' is, the heavier it is and the more it will drag you down and the more topping up it will need. That means more time spent in a negative state and more problems in your life because as we learned through high vibrational thinking all the bad negative stuff is in the lower vibrational zones. That's where it lives, you can't feel anger, hate, jealousy, greed, depression, etc when you are in the higher vibrations, you can only feel these things when your vibration drops down.

Developing 'inner resistance' is nobody's fault and it's something that we all do. Everybody has this it's impossible to not get it. In the world as it is today the experience of negative energy is very much a part of life and impossible to avoid.

This makes 'inner resistance' part of everybody's life. It has an affect on our relationships, health, work, the level of success we can achieve, the amount of money that flows into our life and that we can hold on to, it even controls how happy we can be, it affects everything.

In some people it can manifest as a constant bad mood, flaring up over virtually anything. Making the person a prickly character to be around, lashing out at anybody in the firing line. It even changes the way you look, as the demon within takes you over and lives through you contorting your face in different ways. A beautiful person can change and look ugly when their inner resistance is active and in charge, as their negative feelings shine through.

You often pick up negative behaviour patterns from your parents, maybe one of them was feisty and aggressive in their demeanour and you were repeatedly on the receiving end as a child. This could easily create the same type of inner demon within you, which would leave you with the same behaviour patterns.

A good analogy would be to imagine a slab of butter just out of the fridge so its quite solid and you try to cut into it with a blunt knife, it would be difficult to cut into. Now imagine cutting into the same slab of butter with a red hot sharp knife. It would easily cut deep into the butter. Further still picture the red hot sharp knife covered in something sticky maybe treacle and then dipped in soot. The treacle and soot represents negativity and you can now see when the knife cuts through the butter it would leave dirt deep within the butter.

This is how our mind works, when we are young and especially when we are under six-years old negative experiences cut deep into our supple and impressionable young mind and each deep cut leaves a residue of negative energy, it leaves dirt buried in our mind. The deeper the cut the more negativity is left within us. It becomes embedded deep within us and this is what forms our inner resistance.

Imagine a three-year old in the room when his parents are having a terrible argument. Anger, hate, frustration and fear would be flashing across the room like bolts of lightening and these negative energies would cut through the child like a hot knife through butter. This would leave a deep impression and residue left from those energies would be forever implanted into the child. This is how we pick it up from early experiences in our lives. Then we are stuck with it for life.

Then it manifests through us as we start to show the traits of anger and frustration etc. It has us and it will replenish itself through us when the opportunity arises. It can simply maintain its presence within us or as in many cases grow more powerful.

As we get older we harden up and it's harder for negativity to cut this deep into us. This is why the experiences of our early years in general define the rest of our lives. Deeply buried emotionally charged negative energy becomes lodged within us and we then spend the rest of our lives feeding it and of course this is the more difficult negative energy to get out of us. We become a slave to the negativity that we were subject to in our early years.

The pain of our parents is passed onto to us and it then becomes our pain. Their inner resistance manifesting through them cuts deep into us, then we take on that very energy and it begins to manifest through us. This is how we inherit our parent's negative traits, temper, anger, self-hatred, fear, negative opinions around money etc. Then we have children and pass it on to them, the never ending cycle of inner resistance creating more inner resistance continues, as we unknowingly damage our children. This gives them a more difficult life path to follow, a life in a lower vibration than they need to be.

This is the inner resistance that we all have and end up struggling with in some form or other for the rest of our lives.

Really it doesn't matter how it got there we have all got it, at this point it's no big deal how we got it, your focus now needs to be on getting rid of it. Dwelling on how you got it simply puts the demon in charge, as you play into its hands feeling sorry for yourself or whatever. Forget that and concentrate on solving the problem.

To change your life for the better you must weaken and get rid of your 'inner resistance'. You must get rid of this heavy slow vibrating energy that has got stuck in your energy field and dragged you down. It is holding you at a set vibrational level, like a balloon that is being held under water. Get rid of it and you will rush to the surface, just like the balloon would if you released it.

Otherwise nothing will change; you will live your life stuck at a set vibration because of your 'inner resistance', getting the same problems and niggles day after day. You will be experiencing the same negative feelings and emotions over and over every day of your life.

Anger, frustration, irritation, impatience, envy, disappointment, worry and fear etc will be bouncing in and out of your mind over just about anything; a never ending merry go round of negative thinking and feeling, trapping you in the lower vibrations and making your life more difficult in the process.

This is what most people are chained to all of their lives but that doesn't have to happen to you.

'No one is born hating another person because of the colour of his skin
or his background or his religion. People learn to hate and if they can learn to hate they can be taught to love, for love comes more naturally to the human heart than it's opposite'.

-Nelson Mandela-

South African anti-apartheid revolutionary, politician, and philanthropist, who served as President of South Africa from 1994 to 1999.

Wonderful words by Nelson Mandela, hate or inner resistance is what we are taught and unknowingly accept into our minds. This is not natural to us, love is natural to us and therefore teaching ourselves to love will come much easier than teaching ourselves to hate.

Understanding how your inner resistance works is the first step and then you can work on getting rid of it and replacing it with love (high vibrational energy). This means cut back on the negative thinking and change it to more high vibrational thinking. Thinking and feeling that encapsulates high vibrational energies such as love, consideration, compassion, sincerity, honesty truth etc.

This is how you teach yourself to love. Detach from the negative thoughts and feelings and practice embodying the higher vibrational thoughts and feelings, raising your energy vibration in the process.

It's your inner resistance that is holding you away from the 'high zone' and most of the time this traps you in a lower vibrational place, which in turn messes with your form on the golf course. The 'high zone' is in fact a word describing the higher vibrations where less negativity can infect your game and I believe this is a better description of where you really are when you have the magic and can play way beyond your normal level. The lower down your inner resistance drags you the harder it is to play golf at your best.

It is your inner resistance that is keeping you stuck at a certain level, the amount of success that you have is determined by your vibrational level. Many golfers' amateurs and professionals have been caught in this trap and can't step up to the next level because of the negative influence of their inner resistance. They need to raise their vibration to allow success to flow into their lives; this is what is keeping tournament wins and getting that handicap down just out of reach. And this is what sabotages them from the inside when they do get the opportunity to step up to the next level.

They will feel like they have hit invisible barriers and will convince themselves its other things, their putting, driving, short game, clubs, shoes, bad luck etc but it is not any of these things. It's their inner resistance and it's their inner resistance that will push thoughts into their mind blaming this and that for their lack of success.

This keeps them looking in the wrong place for answers and plays right into the hands of their inner resistance. This ensures its survival at their expense then it can quietly go about its daily business of recharging itself unnoticed and this keeps them well and truly stuck.

If you want to fulfil your potential and achieve more success on the golf course start getting rid of your inner resistance and get your vibration up. You must regain control of your mind.

Chapter 3

The 'High Zone'

"You swing your best when you have the fewest things to think about."

-Bobby Jones-

Robert Tyre "Bobby" Jones Jr. was an American amateur golfer, and a lawyer by profession, who was one of the most influential figures in the history of the sport

To play golf at your very best or indeed any sport you must know how to get into the 'zone', the zone of peak performance, looking through HVT eyes as I mentioned previously I feel 'the high zone' better describes where you actually are, which is **'in the higher vibrations'**.

Even the world's best professional golfers are very rarely in the 'high zone'. The appearance of their absolute best form happens occasionally but not very often. Most of the time they are playing below that level but still playing incredible golf. They can shoot a 61 or 62 or even better when they hit the 'high zone' but generally they are averaging around 71 or 72 a full ten shots adrift. For amateurs the difference can be even greater say 20 shots difference between their normal level and high zone level golf.

Now I am sure everybody has felt this elusive 'form' on rare occasions in whatever sport you may have played. It's the day when you can't seem to put a foot wrong and everything goes for you, 'the luck of the bounce', 'the run of the green', it's magical really when this happens.

Imagine if you could do this all of the time. This is what sports psychologist are paid vast sums of money for, to get their player or players in the 'high zone'. They know some things seem to help, 'leave your last shot behind you', 'stay relaxed', 'visualise the perfect shot' etc but they don't know exactly how or why it works and they don't know how to get there at will.

In recent years there is one golfer who seems to have been better at doing this than all of the rest, Tiger Woods of course. I believe his self-belief has been so strong that this kept the negative energy or doubts out and allowed him to play closer to the 'high zone' more often than everybody else. In fact even though he appears to be the best at getting in the 'high zone' he still does lots of things that can lose him the vibration. I believe this book would even benefit Tiger one of the greatest golfers, if not the greatest that we have ever seen. Imagine what he would be capable of then? I also believe his slip in form in recent years is due to the appearance of negativity in other areas of his life dragging him down slightly in vibration away from the 'high zone', away from the higher vibrations.

HVT holds the key to understanding what the 'high zone' really is and how to attain it at will. It's the last piece of the jigsaw, when HVT is introduced it all falls into place.

What is the 'High Zone'?

In the high zone you feel serene, calm and happy with an overwhelming sense of inner peace and this is the secret to achieving peak performance. This is the mindset you naturally embody when you are in the 'high zone', in other words you are embodying a state of mind that is negative energy free. You are vibrating at the higher levels. No anger, fear, apprehension, doubts, frustration, exasperation, tension, worry or stress etc, all you can feel is peace, serenity happiness, joy and bliss.

If you are a professional or amateur golfer this is the mindset you must always be looking to attain when you are playing golf. To play at your very best you must hold the correct mindset, the mindset of the 'high zone'.

The 'high zone' is quite simply put a state of mind that is free from negative energy of any kind. No negative thoughts, no negative feelings, a calm relaxed state of mind that shimmers with high vibrational positive energies. You can often feel a bubbling up inside of happiness when you find yourself in or close to the 'high zone'.

When you are in the 'high zone' because you are to all intents and purposes negative energy free this means you are also free from your normal negative limiting beliefs and expectations. You leave behind what you perceive is possible and you move into a mindset where you are capable of anything; this is when you can conjure up shots that will astound you as everything seems to miraculously go your way.

You feel serene, calm, tranquil and slightly detached from what you are doing. You are still doing what you need to do but your overriding feeling is a sense of calmness. You are at peace. It feels like you are flowing with the energies and in perfect harmony with your surroundings. You feel relaxed and totally loose, inside you are basking in serenity while still going about all the things you have to do on the outside to play your shot. Your swing is free and easy and you sense there is nothing within you to disturb that.

It almost feels like you are playing through a haze of tranquillity, as you enjoy the calm, peaceful energies. The sense of peace is so powerful that it engulfs you and it feels like you are giving very little attention to the actual shot itself but you feel an undeniable sense of trust that it will work out, and boy does it. You are as we say playing on 'feel', playing on instinct and as you play each shot you are aware of a distinct lack of doubt, a sort of certainty comes over you that you will hit a good shot.

This feeling of certainty has arisen because you are vibrating at a very fast rate out of reach of any negative energy, all the tension (negative energy) has left your body and your swing is completely fluent and free. And as I said before it's like you are not really concentrating on your swing it just happens, you are more immersed in the feelings of inner peace and serenity that are swirling around.

Holding this inner peace and serenity is the key to keeping the form going; this keeps you in the highest possible vibration and brings to you the best possible results because you are above and out of reach of the slower vibrating negative energy.

You are in such a high vibrational place that negative energy is no where to be seen, it can't exist there. You are above it, you are vibrating at a higher frequency and this shows in your golf, as you are able to play perfect shot after perfect shot. You could say you are playing high frequency golf that is free from negative interference.

Just casually picture how you want your shot to go and hold the feelings of serenity and inner peace. Know that it will work out as best as it can for you, as long as you hold this high vibrational state of mind.

If you feel resistance (negative energy) sneaking into your mind through your thoughts and feelings this means you are dropping in vibration away from the 'high zone' and this increases the chances of a less desirable result.

Disappointment, exasperation, irritation, apprehension, worry, anxiety, tension, anger, frustration, doubt, fear and stress are some of the many ways negative energy creeps in and when it gets hold of you your ability to perform at your best is becoming impaired. You cannot perform at your peak when this happens because your vibration is falling; you are dropping down in frequency away from the high vibrations of the 'high zone'. To hold your form you must be aware of your mindset at all times and try not to become entangled in any negative emotions and feelings.

If you do become entangled you can feel your inner peace slipping away as turbulent low vibrational energy subtly enters the equation. You may even just sense it as a slight shimmer but that's enough to drag you down a fraction and impair the quality of your shot. This is where you are normally playing your golf from, an altogether lower vibration with more negative energy around hence the lower performances.

I know I have certainly felt it on occasion when playing in a club competition, an underlying feeling of mild anxiety creeps in and you just can't put your shots together. It doesn't have to be a major tournament just something with a little more importance for you and the next thing you are having a really bad day.

In fact you may not even be able to sense the negative energy at all because it has been part of your being for so long it has become your natural state of being, an ever so slight mild ripple below the surface, barely detectable. This is the mindset that most people are living their lives from. It's only when you understand how it works and know what's happening when you experience total serenity and inner peace that you have a 'high zone' reference point to compare it with, that's when you can learn to feel it.

You must train yourself to be alert and aware so that you can sense negative energy when it subtly appears. Then you must learn how to detach from it, allowing it to be without buying into it. Allow it to drift through your mind and don't try to push it away. Accept its presence without losing your sense of inner peace, this is how you handle it, then it will drift away without hurting you. You notice it without engaging it and you do this while holding the feeling of serenity and inner peace constant.

Don't fight against it or try to push it away because then it has you, you have fallen into the trap, you must be the gentle but detached observer. Once you engage it you are recharging your inner resistance and that is what it wants. It has tricked you into becoming emotionally entangled and that's bad for your golf and you are falling down the vibrations.

The high vibrational mindset you adopt to enter the high zone is not your everyday mindset, not your natural state of being, not your default setting and this is why it is so difficult to hold onto. Everything inside of you is pulling you away from the high zone down to your natural vibrational setting but to play golf of the highest level you must learn how to hold the highest vibrational mindset possible.

You must enter a state of mind that is not normal for you.

Training yourself to hold the correct mindset is the secret; this is the key to peak performance. This should be your daily work, the more you practice the better you will get. This is equally as important as practicing your physical golf shots and the key to consistently being able to produce higher levels of performance. You must practice holding yourself in the higher vibrations. You can do this as you go about your daily activities outside of golf as negativity arises, watch it and don't let it draw you in.

There is absolutely no place for any form of negativity on the golf course, frustration and anger are two of the common negative emotions seen everyday on golf courses around the world. As soon as you allow these demons to take over your mind and become you, you are plummeting in vibration. And that means little things can start going against you, instead of for you. Unless of course you are coming from an even more negative place such as depression then the emotion of anger when you engage it may even pull you up slightly and seem to help for a while but this is not a place to play golf from. The high vibrations are where you want to be to play your best golf.

In the 'high zone' the ball teeters on the edge of the hole for what seems an eternity and then miraculously drops in (like Tigers famous chip) or you hit it into bunker and it gets a freaky lucky bounce and ends up three inches from the hole. When you are in the lower vibrational zones the ball stays out of the hole or plugs in the bunker. **It's not luck; it's your vibrational rate being reflected back to you.**

If you can train yourself to hold the 'high zone' or stay as close to it as possible at all times your game will come on leaps and bounds. You will be able to produce your best form more consistently. You will be able to play negativity free shots and that's the key to peak performance. You will be luckier or it will seem that you are when in fact it is not luck at all; it is working out for you because negative energy is not in the equation to spoil things.

An outburst of anger or a display of frustration means you have engaged negative energy and it has got hold of you, then it is back in the equation. Suddenly you are not lucky anymore, things are not working out and little things go against rather than for you.

How many players have we seen have angry outbursts, even top professionals are doing it? This is causing major damage to their mindset and plunging them down from the higher vibrations away from the 'high zone' into more difficult negative vibrations where everything will be fractionally harder. These are not the mental playing conditions you want to put yourself in.

You only have to look at examples of top players who have had negative situations going on in their private lives and as a result their form on the golf course has suffered. I could name many top professionals that have gone through divorce or relationship difficulties or other outside personal problems and this negative energy that they were subject to in their personal lives hampered their ability when playing golf.

It dragged them down from their normal vibrational level and as a result their form suffered. They were distracted by what was going on in their mind as they tussled with their thoughts and feelings. Negative energy was grabbing hold of them and they couldn't settle it down and relax, they lost their normal vibrational level due to the extra negative energies circulating within and their form suffered accordingly because as you now know the more negative energy that you have in your mind the harder it is to play golf.

And this drop in vibration can last for weeks, months or even years if they do not resolve the issue that is causing it and get their vibration back up. It makes you into a different person, a more negative person in every way and this reflects right across your life as well as in your ability to play golf.

You must become a mind master on the golf course, at peace, serene, tranquil and in control of your emotions at all times. During your round you must have total control and discipline and in time with practice you will not even feel the urge to be negative. Now you are not just thinking about the technicalities of the game but you are also thinking about the mindset you are in. This new way of mentally approaching your golf is how you master the ability to get in the zone.

Tiger Woods may have benefitted from this type of training as a child from his parents, apparently he meditated and this will have helped him learn how to attain the correct peaceful mindset that is conducive to attaining the 'high zone'. This could explain why he can often play at a higher level than everybody else. The majority of us didn't get that type of training at an early age and were subject to whatever energies were around.

This early years training especially up to seven years old is so important, it's when your mind is susceptible to teaching and readily absorbs everything. This forms your vibrational comfort zones and your subconscious mind spends the rest of your life trying to keep you within those comfort zones.

To most of us it's far from natural; we are used to our mind racing with thoughts about all kinds of things. Even when we are relaxing our mind can be bouncing from one thing to another, experiencing all kinds of energies and fully engaging them.

For the majority of us we will have been subject to a 'normal' first seven years, where we will have experienced no mediation classes and taught that it is perfectly normal to fully engage whatever negative energies that came along. A typical family environment will have experienced many forms of negativity, anger, frustration, stress, doubt, the odd argument etc. Even television programs can be very negative and we will have watched them without realising they were damaging us. 'The Soaps' now for example, are full of shouting and screaming, anger and frustration.

This is how it happens and we have no idea it is taking place. It's nobody's fault it's just the way things are. The only problem is your early years programming is hurting you now, it's pulling your vibration down and messing with your form. Tiger just may be lucky enough to have less of it programmed into his subconscious; this could be why he is so good. This may be his secret he naturally is able to stay in the higher vibrations and closer to the high zone because he carries less inner resistance than most.

So while our subconscious mind is programmed to lean towards the negative always pulling us down the vibrations his may be programmed to lean the other way and always pull him up the vibrations.

The good thing is that's all about to change because using HVT I can teach you how to re-program your subconscious mind or to put it another way get rid of your inner resistance and get into the 'high zone' more often. The first step is understanding the concept of HVT, this alone will improve your game. Now you have a different perspective and this automatically empowers you to have more control over negative energy and more control over your emotions. This will instinctively keep you at a higher vibration as you manage negative energy better and that means a less negative mindset so better golf more consistently.

Now you know how it all works, you will be aware when negativity rears its ugly head. This awareness will have a positive impact on how you handle it, which in turn will keep you at a higher vibrational level and therefore a higher performance level. And now you also know what the 'high zone' is and how it feels when you are in it so you know where you need to be, you know what you are looking for.

The three elusive questions have been answered. What is the 'zone', how do you get there and why can you play so well when you are there?

The following ten modules are techniques to help you break down your inner resistance and release it and to get you into a 'high zone' mindset and keep you there or as close to it as possible.

Chapter 4

Ten Modules to attain the 'High Zone'

"There are no shortcuts on the quest for perfection."

-Ben Hogan-

William Ben Hogan was an American professional golfer, generally considered one of the greatest players in the history of the game

Introduction

The Ten Modules are designed to be user friendly and easy to incorporate into your day and life. Re-training your subconscious mind and working on getting rid of your inner resistance is the objective and this will take time, you have spent all of your life up until now living at the mercy of your inner resistance, so it will be well entrenched within your thinking processes. It manifests as your instinctive reactions to whatever events unfold. You miss a three-foot putt; you automatically feel frustration, annoyance or possibly just an uncomfortable sinking feeling in your solar plexus.

This is how it works, you react to something that happens without any conscious thought, you just experience the negative thoughts and feelings. You are programmed to constantly pull yourself down from the 'high zone' because you are a slave to the needs of your inner resistance.

The chances are you don't even know you are doing it; you are just locked into a never ending series of automatic negative habitual reactions and these reactions are continuously recharging your inner resistance. This is keeping you away from the 'high zone' and in the process the majority of the time, holding your very best form on the golf course just out of reach. This is why you only very occasionally experience the magic of the high zone.

You are too busy locked in a dance with your inner resistance and this is all going on inside of your head, most of the time without you even being aware of it.

The Ten Modules will begin the process of releasing your inner resistance and changing the way that you automatically react and think. In time if you have the experience of missing a three-foot putt, you will feel no disturbance to your inner peace, you will be in control. You will not have an instinctive negative reaction. This means you will be doing no damage to your energy vibration and therefore ensuring that you stay at the highest possible vibration throughout your round, as well as giving less power to your inner resistance thus continually weakening it in the process.

The result is you will begin rising in vibration and that means your golf will improve and you will be able to play more consistently at a higher level. Remember the higher your vibration is the closer you are to the 'high zone' and the better golf you can play.

The Ten Modules or at least some of them should become part of your life, a discipline that you follow everyday and thanks to HVT giving you a new perspective this will not be something that you should find difficult to implement. The shift in thinking that is required has already begun with the absorption of the basic principles of HVT and the understanding you now have about how your inner resistance works. Now I will add to that momentum with the Ten Modules, which are specifically designed to gently but powerfully encourage positive changes within your subconscious programming and lessen the effect of your inner resistance on your habitual thinking patterns this will help you attain the 'high zone' more easily and more naturally.

All you have to do is absorb the information and allow it to happen, a small amount of action is required on your part following some of the Ten Modules but you can keep this to manageable levels. Overloading you with extra work and routines is a sure way to fail because then you create inner turmoil, which is exactly what we are trying to leave behind. Keeping it simple is the key and HVT allows us to create simple routines that don't get in the way and still get the job done.

The difference between your current level and stepping up to the next level is taking control of your mind and harnessing that power. You have got to the level you are today without doing that and have in fact been held back by your mind. Can you imagine to what heights you can now soar in your golf career whether you are amateur or professional now that you know how it works and what to do? Your true potential can now be realised, there is no limit to what you can now go on to achieve.

Modules 1 to 3 are exercises that you can build into your everyday life and they will begin the process of breaking down and getting rid of your inner resistance permanently. This will raise your vibration making it easier for you to get yourself up and into the 'high zone' when required. Because obviously you will be existing naturally at a higher vibrational level closer to the 'high zone' as well as having less inner resistance dragging you down.

Modules 4 to 10 are best used when you are playing or preparing to play to get your vibration up into the 'high zone' for your round.

Chapter 5

General Modules to break down your inner resistance

Module 1

"What we think we become"

-Buddha-

Gautama Buddha, also known as Siddhārtha Gautama or simply the Buddha, after the title of Buddha, was an ascetic and sage, on whose teachings Buddhism was founded.

Notebook Method

I advocate everybody uses this module in your everyday life to begin the process of breaking down your inner resistance and getting your vibration up. This will familiarise you with the many different energies that you experience on a daily basis. It will teach you how to recognise the feelings of the 'high zone' as well as the feelings of not being in the 'high zone'. This is vitally important so that when you are playing golf you can feel your way to the 'high zone' when need be.

Get yourself a small notebook to write down every time that you feel yourself becoming negative. Writing is a wonderful form of therapy and an important part of your re-programming. Keep your notebook with you at all times and write down everything that creates negative feelings within you. It maybe a comment from your partner, a look at your financial situation, you reacting to your random thoughts, a missed putt, a wayward drive or even just forgetting your golf shoes.

Whatever it is, write it down and you will soon form a picture of how your inner resistance is functioning (it may be prudent just to acknowledge your negative feelings when playing golf and jot them down later).

You see if a situation arises like you forgetting your golf shoes you don't have to fall into negative feelings, anger, frustration etc. That is just the programming (your inner resistance) drawing you in. Of course you may have to go home for your shoes but do it without the frustration and anger; you have to do it anyway.

Your focus should always be serenity and inner peace. The trick is just to accept it and stay in a peaceful state of mind, the choice is yours. Remember serenity and inner peace means better more consistent golf.

You are by following this practice learning to monitor your thinking and the fact that you are interrupting your negative thinking when it occurs actually diffuses its power. Every time you notice it, its power diminishes and in time you will not even have negative thoughts. You are re-training your mind and in the process holding your vibration up closer to the 'high zone' making it easier for you to slip into the 'high zone' when playing golf.

Entries may look something like this:

*Gas bill arrived I felt a **sinking** feeling.*

*Got caught on a speed camera I was **angry.***

*Thinking about Christmas I feel **worried** about money.*

*Noisy motorbike outside house it really **irritated** me.*

*No milk in fridge I am **frustrated**.*

*Thinking about that incident last week, I am **annoyed**.*

*Missed three-foot putt I felt **gutted**.*

*Hit my drive out of bounds was **angry**.*

As you can see there are thousands of little niggles that could pop up and most of the time when this happens we allow ourselves to feel some form of negativity, we just do it automatically. This is what you must stop. It's this daily engaging in negative energy that is keeping the negative energy that dwells within you alive. You are topping up its battery all of the time and this is what is keeping you away from the 'high zone'. Writing down every time you experience yourself engaging negative energy stops you from giving it a full emotional charge.

It is the emotionally fuelled charge that tops up the negative energy within you and keeps it strong. Stopping that charge in its tracks will weaken the negative energy within you and eventually eradicate it all together. You will find that when you do feel the urge to react to something it's less severe than it used to be. Something that previously really enraged you will hardly even annoy you. This shows you that you are carrying less negative energy within you, which in turn allows your energy vibration to rise and settle at a new higher level.

The more you train yourself not to react and more importantly not to feel the emotional surge (anger, frustration, disappointment etc) the weaker your inner resistance will become. The slow vibrational heavy energy will become lighter and allow you to rise in vibration and that means everything will be better including your form on the golf course.

The fact that you can carry your notebook with you and it is tangible and real on the physical level gives you an easy to use tool. This is your first step in re-programming your subconscious mind and stepping your golf up to the next level. Couple this practice up with some of the other modules that suit you and you will be astounded at how quickly you progress.

Chapter 6

Module 2

"I have to believe in myself. I know what I can do, what I can achieve."

-Sergio Garcia-

Sergio García Fernández is a Spanish professional golfer who plays on both the PGA Tour and the European Tour he has won The Masters and more than 30 other international tournaments as a professional

Note for Sergio Garcia in respect of The Masters 2017:

"Congratulations Sergio you had to break through those inner barriers to land this one after coming close so many times a testimony to your inner strength and resolve. I am so pleased for you and I am sure you will now go on to win many more Majors well done".....Steve Wharton

Inner Child

I believe this module is one of the most important and beneficial of all the ten techniques. Understanding how your inner child operates and working on changing that is paramount in order for you to get the best from all of the other modules. Without employing this technique whatever you try will always be thwarted to some degree by your inner child's efforts to keep you within your vibrational comfort zones.

Your inner child

The eminent psychologist Sigmund Freud discovered that our subconscious mind is like a small child. He called it the inner child and found that it pretty much resembles what you were like at 5 or 6 years old. If you can imagine yourself at five-years old then that is a good way to picture your inner child. This child that lives inside you functions mainly on the data it was fed in the first 5 or 6 years of your life.

This early year's data or program can be very limiting because your subconscious mind (inner child) regards this early years programming as home, or your comfort zones. It then spends the rest of your life monitoring you and keeping you within those comfort zones. It's really a vibrational comfort zone, an average vibrational level. And your inner child wants to maintain your vibration at this familiar level and it will manipulate you in anyway that it can to keep you within those vibrational boundaries.

The more powerful your inner resistance is the lower your vibrational comfort zone will be. In other words the more inner negativity you are carrying the further down the vibrations it will drag you. So therefore the harder it will be to get up into the 'high zone' and hold yourself there.

Let's take another brief look at how this early years programming works

You may be brought up in a negative environment filled with arguments, fear, a feeling of lack, an underprivileged neighbourhood, a family that experiences money troubles, poverty, negative minded parents, lack of parental love and even violence. This sets the vibrational level for your subconscious mind and with all of that negative energy flying around you would be lucky on a scale of 1-10 to end up better than 2 or 3. This becomes your comfort zone and basically where your subconscious will try to keep you for the rest of your life. This would be a slow negative vibration that you have effectively through your early year's life experience become chained to.

Not many world class golfers or successful people will come from this type of background. In fact most of the people from this type of negative background will end up having a life filled with problems. They will age quicker, be ill more, have more accidents and misfortune and in general struggle in many areas of their life. Their inner child will be conditioned to maintain their vibrational level and hold them in an existence filled with problems pandering to the demands of their inner resistance. The hassle and problems abound in the lower vibrational levels.

I am sure some very talented golfers do come from this type of background but they will most likely have failed well before they managed to get anywhere near realising their potential. Sabotage from within by their subconscious mind and inner resistance is usually far too powerful to ignore and often they end up believing everybody has it in for them or they lose motivation and give up trying. When in actual fact the only thing really working against them comes from within their own mind.

Then you have a 'normal' childhood experience, caring parents, the odd argument, average neighbourhood, reasonable lifestyle, enough money but not an abundance, not too negative parents. This would give you say a 5 or 6 level. This is where the majority of golfers will have come from. This type of conditioning would be what most of us have experienced.

Then you have the exceptionally positive childhood, an abundance of love, nice home environment, positive parents, and few household problems creating a nice high vibrational home. This is where you would probably have parents that encourage self-love and self-belief giving you the best possible start in life and from here you might end up at 8 or 9 level. Now you have had a great start and you are free to achieve your potential or come close. This is where you would end up naturally existing at a high vibrational level with less inner resistance to pull you down and find it easier to move up and into the 'high zone' when playing golf. Possibly this is the type of childhood Tiger Woods had.

Of course this is not an exact science many personal traits determine how you will evolve, sensitivity, personality, temperament, strength of character, intelligence etc. Everybody handles things differently and one person may find a difficult negative childhood destroys them and they end up having a miserable unhappy life. Whereas another person from exactly the same background may have the determination, focus and willpower to forge on to a successful and happy life. However in general the majority will never break free from their vibrational conditioning set in childhood. Our early year's data download will dominate our entire life and hold us with the help from our inner child at a set vibrational level. The lower that level the more difficult our life will be.

The inner child likes what is familiar and has no conception of whether this is good or bad for you. All it knows is that you have a vibrational setting and its job is to keep you within those boundaries. It operates automatically and when you threaten to move out of the set vibration it clicks into action. This is where self-doubts come from, that little voice in your head gets to work. 'I hope I don't shank it', 'I'd better not under hit it', 'that out of bounds looks close', 'what if I win', 'I'm not good enough', 'I don't deserve it', 'Can I really beat these good players' etc.

Anything that has the potential to bring you success at any level (in other words pull you up the vibrations) will more than likely trigger a surge in negative thinking. Self-doubt, worry, fear, lack of motivation and even injury are some of the ways that your inner child will try to sabotage your success and keep you in your comfort zone. Even winning your club monthly medal can result in an attack from within.

Every golfer and indeed every person will have experienced this many times, it is part and parcel of golf at every level. You know how your pals try to put you off, 'watch out for that bunker', 'your tee looks a little high', 'there are a lot of trees around here'. Sure enough as soon as the thought is implanted you end up doing it, well that's exactly how your subconscious works, only this time it's coming from inside your head an even more powerful form of suggestion.

Your inner child does not want you to move out of your programmed vibration and if winning a tournament or being more successful than usual will do this, it will try to stop you. This monitoring extends into every area of your life not just golf. Whatever you are involved in, work, relationships or sport it will impose its influence and try to keep you in the comfort zone, in the vibrational frequency range it has been programmed with.

As soon as you threaten to move up in vibration (maybe win your playing card, win a big tournament or for an amateur golfer win the club competition) you could well experience any of the following tactics to keep you from success: self-doubt, lack of motivation, illness, injury, bad luck, anxiety, worry, stress etc. Anything can happen and usually does; your inner child is very inventive in the multitude of ways that it can halt your progress. Yes it can even attract injury to get what it wants.

Jonny Wilkinson was in my opinion a classic subconscious induced injury case. When he dropped the goal to win England the Rugby World Cup he effectively elevated himself to superstar status. This singled him out as England's hero and he became the centre of attention for the world's media. This extra attention and success that was heaped upon him was I believe too much for his subconscious (inner child) to handle and it was backed into a corner.

The magnitude of his drop goal was rocketing him up in vibration and his inner child didn't like it one bit. It had to stop him at all costs and get him back down into the comfort zone, back to the vibrational range it was used to and I am sure it tried many tactics but in the end the only thing that was going to stop the vibrational rise was injury. Sure enough Jonny got injured soon after the World Cup and was dragged from the limelight. Over the following year he hardly played and was pulled back towards his comfort zone, back out of the limelight, back to where his inner child wanted him, back into the grip of his inner resistance.

Sounds incredible to think that your inner child can even make you get injured but it certainly can and it will use this if it has to, to get what it wants. Your inner child is immensely powerful and can create anything it wants, so can you imagine if you could harness that power rather than have it working against you. Your potential can only really be realised when you achieve this. I have no doubt whatsoever that Jonny Wilkinson would not have been plagued by injury in the year after the World Cup if he had not dropped the crucial winning goal.

And I am equally certain that many very talented sportsmen have had their career wrecked by injury problems created by their inner child. When your talent exceeds your subconscious programming comfort success level you will have an inner battle to succeed and achieve your potential. A battle that you will lose if you don't understand what's happening.

There will be thousands of professional golfers around the world blessed with amazing natural talent unable to achieve their potential due to this phenomenon. They will have shown what they can do at various levels and been touted as stars of the future but it never happened. They hit their inner limitations imposed by their own subconscious mind. The most difficult barriers they must overcome are inside their own head.

These barriers or comfort zones are monitored and patrolled by their inner child (subconscious mind) and this is what is really holding them back. Golf courses around the world are littered with immensely talented golfers who had the ability to win majors but were never able to get past what was going on in their own mind and the main reason for that was the didn't fully understand it so were unable to overcome it.

What can you do?

To get control of your inner child you must first understand how it operates in respect of monitoring your vibrational frequency and then you must make contact and build a relationship with the goal being to get it on your side.

'The mind game finally explained'

Most people will not even be aware that they have an inner child let alone know how it operates. Now you know how it works we can look at how to meet your inner child and start building the relationship, which will enable you to enlist its power for you instead of blindly struggling against it.

Meeting your inner child is done with a simple visualisation and it can be very emotional the first time that you do this. My first experience happened many years ago when my father died. I was thirty-seven years old and I was of course upset and feeling the grief associated with losing a loved one. However this grieving went 'on and on' and after a few months it became obvious that I was slipping into depression.

I looked everywhere for help, hypnotherapy, bereavement workshops, counseling and nothing worked. I didn't know where to turn then I came across a book referring to Sigmund Freud's work in respect of the inner child. I thought 'this is it' all of my efforts were focused on making me the adult feel better, the conscious mind.

When I was actually fine it wasn't me that was overwhelmed with grief it was my inner child, my subconscious mind. I had given all the attention to me and none to him. All along the pain inside me was my inner child, upset and feeling abandoned by his father. This inner pain was dragging me down into depression, into the lower vibrational zones.

I immediately realised that I needed to do a visualisation exercise to connect with my inner child, this was how I could make contact with him. I lay on my bed and closed my eyes then I pictured my inner child upset and sobbing, as any five year old would be after losing his father. I took him up into my arms and gave him a big cuddle and I explained that I would love and look after him from now on. I took him into the park and we played on the swings, I saw him happy and smiling, the sobbing stopped and he was happy again. I even brought my father into the visualisation and saw the three of us enjoying the moment.

I stayed with this visualisation for about ten minutes and when I got up off the bed I was completely cured. The inner pain was gone and I felt back to my normal self. It was miraculous the transformation that had taken place. Months of depression blown away in ten minutes. The depression never returned and I made a decision from that day forward to connect with my inner child on a regular basis to reassure him that I love him.

What had actually happened is the negative feelings that were engulfing my inner child, hurt, sadness, anger, pain and fear were dragging me down into the lower vibrations. My visualisation changed the way my inner child was feeling from sad to happy and this released the inner negativity and I was able to rise back up to my normal vibrational level.

The heavy negative energy created by my inner child's state of mind slipped away and as a result I rose in vibration.

Loving your inner child is the key and all you need to do is a simple ten minute visualisation to make the connection. By loving him you are helping him break free from the vibrational conditioning. Love is the most powerful high vibrational energy in the universe and when you love your inner child you are dissolving the negative energy that he is being controlled by.

Technique for your round

In respect of golf having your inner child in as happy a mindset as possible will always help you play better because it keeps you in the higher vibrations. Here is a visualisation that you can use before you play your round. Preferably before you set off for the golf course set aside ten minutes to relax and do your visualisation. You can lie on the bed, relax in a comfortable chair or you could even do this exercise sat in your car.

Close your eyes and picture your inner child, you at five-years old. Reach down and pick up your inner child and give him or her a big hug. This exercise is all about love and affection because introducing that energy to your inner child will help raise your vibration putting you in the best vibrational place for your round.

Tell your inner child that you love him/her, feel the love between you both as you hug him/her. The more you can actually create the feeling of love the more powerful the exercise. Love will dissolve the negative energy that binds your inner child to the early years programming. See your inner child happy and full of fun, running around giggling. It's all about introducing as much positive energy as possible, feeling it is the key.

When your inner child is joyful and happy you can tell him/her about the round of golf you are going to play and how much fun it will be. Keeping the fun element in your golf is important because this is again high vibrational energy. Ask your inner child to help you play well and give him/her some incentive maybe you will treat them to a bag of sweets (which of course you will eat), a trip to the cinema, a DVD or even a holiday. The child element in you (your inner child) is what you are pleasing. I am sure we all enjoy movies like 'Back to the Future' and 'Mrs Doubtfire' your inner child will love these kinds of DVD's and they will certainly like the idea of a bag of sweets.

Enlisting the help of your inner child with an incentive means you are directing them away from the vibrational monitoring and giving them something else to focus on. And just like any real child of that age, they love treats and having fun. They will get excited and happy and this is the type of energy that you are looking to generate, this lifts you up. The happier your inner child is the better you will play golf and the easier it will be for you to break free from your comfort zones and achieve your true potential. The happier they are, the easier it is for you to get into the 'high zone' and stay there.

Building your relationship

Keeping in regular contact with your inner child through visualisation is how you can build your relationship. Maybe you could do a simple visualisation every week or even every time you play to make that connection. Five or ten minutes will be enough whatever suits you is fine, it's all about showing your inner child that you love and care for them.

Creating the correct feelings when you do this is important; basking in the love energy will get your inner child used to the higher vibrational energies and help to raise your vibration. The happier your inner child is the happier you are. Happy means less negativity and that means better golf.

This exercise will also pull your inner child away from its duties as monitor of your vibrational rate. Giving you a rest from its constant attention will help you feel release from the lower vibrational energies that you are carrying within your energy field, your inner resistance. All of this will help your vibration and allow it to rise enhancing your golf in the process.

Chapter 7

Module 3

"Forget the last shot. It takes so long to accept that you can't always replicate your swing. The only thing you can control is your attitude toward the next shot."

-Mark McCumber-

Mark Randall McCumber is an American professional golfer who has played on the PGA Tour and Champions Tour

Energy Diffusing

This is a technique used to help break down and release your inner resistance. After many years of habitual negative reactions we end up with strong blockages within our energy field. The point of this exercise is to get rid of those energy blockages using a technique I call 'energy diffusing'.

Blockages are concentrations of heavy negative energy that have become stuck within your energy field. Everybody carries these blockages, it is virtually impossible to live your life without acquiring them. They are created by your many negative experiences and solidified within your energy field by the emotional reactions generated during repeats of those experiences. They are to all intents and purposes trapped emotional energy.

If you can picture your energy field with various sized dark balls of energy dotted here and there, this gives you a good impression of what your inner resistance might look like. These dark balls of negative energy are stuck and exert a negative influence, which spirals out and touches every area of your life.

They are like little weights that hold down your overall vibration making it difficult to lift yourself up the vibrations and into the 'high zone'. Getting rid of the many little negative weights will help you rise in vibration and more easily be able to hold the 'high zone', which as you know is key to peak performance. The less negative blockages you are carrying, the more easily you will be able to attain and hold the correct mindset to play golf at your best.

Energy diffusing technique

Before I explain the technique you need to understand that you have dozens or maybe even hundreds of these negative energy balls lodged within your energy system. Some will be larger and more powerful than others. The really persistent ones can keep on growing in strength depending on how often and how emotionally fired up you get, when they grab your attention. They can get so powerful that they can virtually take you over permanently and you end up living your life through them.

This would be a person that is always angry, depressed, stressed, worried, anxious, tense, frustrated, full of hatred etc. Often when this is the case the pain of living life like this can become unbearable that some people may turn to drugs, alcohol or some other fix just to get through the day.

Fortunately most of us are not that severely affected but we all are definitely affected to a large degree. This technique will help remove the energy balls from your system, some of the more severe ones may take a few sessions.

They can be created in many different ways related to all sorts of subjects. Thoughts around money often sparks off negative feelings, you may worry about not having enough because this is what you picked up as a child from your parents. That worried feeling around money when the subject pops up is the ball of energy within you relating to your beliefs about money sparking into life. Relationships are another subject that often generates negative feelings.

You may have issues with your father or mother, which creates negative feelings within, again this is the ball of energy relating to that particular subject being activated. It could take the form of anger, frustration or maybe just irritation, or of course any other form of negativity mild or strong.

Your looks, your hair, the way you walk, where you live, your car, your weight, your complexion, your clothes, your next door neighbour, your girlfriend or boyfriend, your just about anything can create a ball of negative energy that dwells within you. And when that subject pops up you just get the negative feelings, as the ball of negativity becomes activated.

The more powerfully and emotionally you engage in it, the more you are recharging it and making it stronger. And of course all of this 'normal' behaviour is not going to help you on the golf course when to achieve peak performance you must train yourself to leave it all behind.

Easier said than done when it's all happening on autopilot, you are simply reacting to whatever is going on and it has become habitual. You do it without thinking and this is what you must gain control of if you are to train yourself to attain the high zone and play golf more consistently at your very peak.

Diffusing your inner negative energy can only help your game. You are letting go of heavy weights of energy that are collectively holding down your energy vibration, just like throwing sand bags out of a hot air balloon.

As you release the weight you will rise in vibration making it easier for you to attain the 'high zone' of peak performance. Every ball of negative energy is playing its part in keeping you from the high vibrational mindset you need to be in, to consistently hit lower scores.

The Technique

This is a simple six-step procedure to change a ball of negative energy into a ball of positive energy. Find yourself a quiet moment and sit in a comfortable chair or lay down on your bed. Make sure you won't be disturbed, as you will need five to ten minutes of peace and quiet.

First you must choose which ball of energy to work with and this is done by deciding and thinking about something in particular, then sensing the ball of energy and feeling its presence within you. Maybe you want to focus on your negative feelings relating to money, a certain relationship or possibly an aspect of your game. Let's start with your putting, think of yourself lining up to take a putt and picture the image.

Now you are looking for any ripples of energy anywhere within your body it could be your solar plexus, your head, your chest area, your hands or practically anywhere. When you sense a shimmer of disturbance maybe in the form of tension, anxiety or just a slight flutter you have located where this ball of energy is resident within you. Now picture the ball of energy, it may be small and light grey spinning on its axis or it could be a large as a football, very dark and full of power, swirling and pulsating with aggression.

Visualise the ball and bring it outside of your body, see it floating in the air maybe four or five-feet in front of you. Look at the negative power within the ball as it spins vigorously on its axis. Personify it, give it a name whatever comes to mind will do maybe Igor, Gorteck, Starbik or whatever it's usually an odd gremlin type of name that pops up for me.

In your mind explain to Igor or whoever, that you are going to help him release his negativity and this will make him happy and content rather than being wound up and unhappy. He may even talk back to you at this point, it could be aggressive or thankful and appreciative, just let him speak.

Now tell Igor that you are going to place him into a bathtub full of love energy, pure undiluted love. For the purposes of the visualisation see yourself melt into the bathtub creating the bathtub full of golden nectar love energy, then slowly immerse the ball of energy (Igor) into the tub. Take your awareness above the bath and watch as the ball spins in the tub and then starts to slow down at the same time changing colour from dark to

'The mind game finally explained'

light. Then after a moment it starts to spin the other way and the colour gets lighter and lighter. Igor could end up white, gold, yellow, pink or some other mix of bright positive colours.

When Igor is pulsating a powerful bright light see him float up out of the tub and spin. Thank him for helping you to change him from negative to positive energy and he may thank you back and tell you his new more positive name. He might be called Star or Thor or something else more appropriate to his new identity.

See yourself rise back out of the bath tub and take on your normal physical body then allow the new positive ball of energy to be absorbed back into your body and see white light pulsating from it, as it settles into your being. The light is radiating out all around you illuminating your room.

Enjoy the moment for as long as you like, picturing and feeling the positive energy shimmering through you out into your surroundings. Get used to the feelings that this generates and bask in the serenity and inner peace.

Let's summarise the six-steps for easy implementation.

1. Get comfortable in a quiet place where you won't be disturbed.
2. Choose and picture the particular ball of energy that you want to work on and sense its presence within you.
3. Visualise the ball of energy outside of you and personify it. (give it a name)
4. Immerse the ball of energy in the bath tub of your golden love energy.
5. Bring the new positive ball of energy back into your being.
6. Take a few moments to relax, enjoy and become familiar with the new energy and how it feels.

You can do this exercise anytime you want and, as many times on each subject, as you feel is required. It's a simple visualisation that will begin eradicating negative energy from your system. You are in effect releasing part of your inner resistance and this will make it easier for you to be able to attain the correct mindset on the golf course because you will have less inner negativity trying to get your attention.

Initially I would focus on golf related inner negativity, such as if your confidence dips with your putting, driving or any other

'The mind game finally explained'

aspect of your game and this will get to the source of the problem improving your game in the process.

For example you may be having a confidence issue with say four or five foot putts, this means your inner resistance has developed negative thinking patterns around this part of your game. So every time you are faced with one of these putts it will click into action. You will experience a surge of doubts and uncertainty and this will play into its hands generating negativity maybe in the form of fear, apprehension, uncertainty etc. This then drags your vibration down a touch putting you in a slightly tenser more uneasy negative state and that's all it takes to create a negative result and you end up missing the putt.

After you have worked on golf related inner resistance then you could tackle the usual major negative generators in our lives, money, relationships, success, parents etc.

This technique is a HVT adaption from the old Tibetan practice of 'feeding your demons'. An excellent book is written on this subject called 'Feeding your Demons' by Tsultrim Allione available from Hay House Publishers.

Chapter 8

Golf focussed modules

Module 4

"The game has such a hold on golfers because they compete not only against an opponent, but also against the course, against par, and most surely- against themselves."

-Arnold Palmer-

Arnold Daniel Palmer was an American professional golfer who is generally regarded as one of the greatest and most charismatic players in the sport's history

Driftwood

This simple meditation can be done every day, I prefer mornings as well as just before my round of golf. It will help you to attain the correct mindset and rise up in vibration into the 'high zone'. You can also think about it anytime during your round (or during your day when your not playing golf) to help settle down any negative energy that may have entered your mind or that may be circulating in your immediate vicinity.

Other people will often be generating negative energy, complaining about this or moaning about that and when you are subject to this it is damaging your energy vibration, it is very easy to get caught up in it and engage it without realising. The more emotionally involved you get, the worse that damage will be, always be on your guard against negative energy from others. Even gossiping is recharging your inner resistance therefore hurting your form on the golf course; try not to get involved in it at least not with feelings.

Training yourself to embody the mindset of this meditation will settle the energies and keep you in the highest possible vibration. It's a great way to practice putting yourself in the feeling mindset of the 'high zone' and you can practice it anytime. Although one of my favourite places to do this meditation is in the bath it really helps me to become the piece of driftwood as I feel the water around and underneath me.

Take about 10 to 15 mins for this exercise.

I want you to sit comfortably or lie down for this exercise and close your eyes. Try to relax and imagine that you are a small piece of driftwood floating down a river. It's a beautiful day the sun is shining and the air is still. You can feel the water supporting you as you gently float down the river and the suns rays make you feel warm and comfortable.

Occasionally you sense a slight ripple or current and you flow softly with the river as it eases you in a different direction. You are enjoying the scenes on the riverbank as you observe a family having a picnic and their pet dog playfully barking.

All the time you feel the river underneath you as it winds its way through the beautiful scenery. Birds are singing and the fish swim underneath you, as you drift by. You feel almost invisible but so incredibly alive. The tranquillity of the moment washes over you and you feel serene and at peace. You offer no resistance to the river whatsoever; you simply allow it to take you wherever it chooses. Even when for a brief moment you get caught up in the reeds and come to a stop, you still feel relaxed and at peace. After a short while the current breaks you free from the reeds and your lovely journey continues.

On you go floating with the river and observing the world around you. A soft breeze picks up and suddenly you feel the water gathering speed and you begin bobbing around on the surface carried by the powerful ebb and flow. You still feel completely relaxed and at peace even though the water has become slightly more buoyant. You know that you are completely at the mercy of the elements and you totally accept your place in the scheme of things. You go with the flow and accept whatever comes your way all the time feeling serene and at peace.

Nothing disturbs your wonderful feeling of peace and tranquillity because you are a piece of driftwood that can offer no resistance to whatever comes your way. You are in harmony with nature and absolutely free to just be.

This feeling of non-resistance pervades your very being and you sense a warm glow from within. You are free from relentless thinking and analysing and happy to just be and let life take you, as you fully enjoy the moment. Your inner peace is extending from inside of you out into the universe and you bask in the soft gentle waves of energy that it sends shimmering through you.

You have become the driftwood and surrendered yourself to the elements; this act of surrender has freed you from your usual tussle with your thoughts and allowed you to find your inner peace. Enjoy these feelings for as long as you want, these are the feelings of the 'high zone'. You can extend the meditation and make it up as you go along. I have just given you a brief picture of what you should focus on to create serenity and inner peace.

Become familiar with these feelings because this is the mindset that you need to be able to generate at will in order to play golf at your absolute best. This is the place of serenity and inner peace. On the golf course you should always be reaching for this feeling place because this means you are free from negative energy and able to play unbelievable golf, this is the 'high zone'.

The analogy of the driftwood perfectly conveys the mentality that you should embody as you live each day of your life. You must flow with whatever energies come along and simply allow yourself to be carried with them. Just like the driftwood you should have no resistance, just go with the flow and ride the energies. Resistance means you have engaged negative energy and you will suffer the consequences, you will drop in vibration.

Of course you still have to deal with everyday problems but you do it in a way that does not disturb your inner peace and serenity. Like forgetting your golf shoes, you accept the fact and you go and get them, you do not get frustrated and angry. This is the most efficient way to maintain your energy vibration, remember go with the flow, be like the piece of driftwood and have no resistance to anything that you have to deal with.

This visualisation is designed to get you in the correct 'feeling' place. This is so important and you can practice this anytime you want. Knowing how it feels to be in the 'high zone' gives you a point of reference a 'feeling place' that you can train yourself to remember and the more you practice experiencing the feelings through doing the meditation the better you will get at recreating them. There will also be many other benefits; your life outside golf will improve in every way.

Get used to the word 'Driftwood' let that be your trigger word that clicks you into the higher vibrations and into the 'high zone'. Whenever you feel negative energy think 'Driftwood', train yourself to associate all the high vibrational feelings of serenity, tranquillity and inner peace with that word.

Then when you sense yourself feeling negative just say 'Driftwood' in your mind and allow the accompanying feelings to replace any negative energy that is trying to get your attention. Let it be the key that allows you to fall into the feelings of surrender and let the negative energy simply slip away. Just imagine yourself as the driftwood in a state of complete acceptance of 'what is' and go with the flow without resistance.

Doing the mediation daily will firmly establish the correct feelings within your psyche and stepping back into those feelings using your trigger word will become second nature. You will then be able to use the trigger word to bring yourself back to peace and serenity if you feel negative energy entering your mind on the golf course. The more you practice this the better you will get at doing it.

This is an excellent exercise when you are feeling the pressure maybe over an important putt or when in the running on the back nine. Always remember keep your vibration as high as possible for peak performance.

Clicking into the 'Driftwood' mindset is clicking into the 'high zone' or as near as you can get to it at any given moment. This is a tool that you can cultivate to put yourself in the 'high zone' at any time. Use it as you play your round to bring yourself back to the correct mindset.

Another great way to create a trigger for this mindset is next time you are walking on the beach look for a small piece of driftwood maybe 3 or 4 inches long. Drill a hole in it and put a piece of string through it. Then hold it in your hand when you next do the meditation and afterwards tie it to your golf bag. Then every time you need it just look at it or maybe hold it for a second to remind you of the serene tranquillity and this will help click you into the high zone.

It can become a physical anchor for you to bring you back to inner peace, back into the high zone.

Chapter 9

Module 5

"Golf is about how well you accept, respond to, and score with your misses much more so than it is a game of your perfect shots."

–Dr Bob Rotella–

Dr. Bob Rotella is consistently recognised as the world's premier sports psychologist.

Yellow Dot

During your round of golf you should be always trying to feel and hold yourself in the high vibrational feelings of the 'high zone' or as close to it as possible. This means maintaining your serenity and inner peace is your main priority. You are playing your golf but you feel slightly detached from it, as your predominant focus is on basking in serenity and inner peace. You are playing with no emotional involvement whatsoever in what's happening. Your focus is serenity and inner peace and for the purpose of this module I call this the 'Yellow Dot' technique.

If you hit a bad shot it means nothing to you, it registers nothing within you all you feel is serenity and inner peace, negative energy can't touch you.

You know that to hold your form and play at your absolute best you must maintain this mindset until the very last putt has dropped. Then and only then can you switch off the inner peace and allow your attention to be distracted by other things.

This is how you keep control and play at your very best. It's all about the right mindset and staying in it. You will hit shot after shot that will astound you, as you consistently hit peak form. Your mind is the key and now you know what it takes, you only have to follow the procedures.

In the correct state of mind you will find that you don't have to meticulously analyse every shot so much, it's more of trusting your subconscious to play the perfect shot. You just 'feel' the shot, hold your inner peace and allow it to happen.

Gently picture how you want the shot to go and see it clearly in your mind, then in your relaxed state of serenity and inner peace play the shot. You should feel happy and calm and completely unaffected by how the shot unfolds. If you hit a brilliant shot great, if you hit a bad shot great, it does not cause a ripple on your inner peace either way.

You have by attaining the right mindset and allowing the feeling of being slightly detached took the conscious mind out of the way and allowed the subconscious to take over. This is the secret, bringing the subconscious mind into the game and allowing it to play through you. Your subconscious is immensely powerful and up until now you have only experienced its unlimited ability on very rare occasions.

You may have even by some quirk of circumstances played the odd full round in the correct mindset and that's when you will have played the round of your life and your left wondering what magic visited you on that day. Now you know and you can produce that magic whenever you want if you can learn to hold yourself in the 'high zone'.

Staying detached is the key with no emotional involvement in what's going on. All you want to feel is peaceful, calm and serene.

In this state of mind negativity cannot grab hold of you it can't hurt you.

You are free to play to your potential.

Technique

To get you in the correct detached state of mind I want to give you a simple technique that you can use before and during your round. It's all about taking your mind off golf and onto something that generates the right high vibrational feelings, then holding those feelings for your entire round.

This can be done at home or when you arrive at the golf course I want you to take a few minutes maybe sat in your car or somewhere else quiet to relax and picture the following:

You are on a desert island nobody else is there just you. You are sat on an old worn wooden deck chair looking out over a beautiful turquoise sea. There is a rickety wooden jetty with a multi-coloured rowing boat tethered to it. Dolphins swim playfully in the shallows and pelicans scurry down the beach looking for scraps of fish, as crabs hurry into the water out of their way.

*The sand is perfect white and it feels powdery and light. The sun is a **shining ball of yellow** casting a warm glow all around and you haven't got a care in the world. This truly is your tranquil paradise and you are free from all the usual niggles of life. You smile gently as you sit back and take it all in feeling the warm sun on your face and the ever so gentle breeze coming in off the sea.*

Negativity doesn't exist here you can only feel happy and content. You feel like you are almost floating in the beauty of it all and the sound of the sea swishing softly upon the beach gently sooths you. You almost feel like you are at one with everything and everything is you, you are the dolphins and the warms rays of sunshine. You are in perfect harmony with your surroundings. You are flooded with serenity and inner peace.

When you feel sufficiently peaceful and relaxed you are ready to play your game of golf. Your mind is in the right place and your job is to keep it there throughout your round. The golf is not important, holding your mind in the feeling of paradise is and you need to hold your vibration at this setting for your round.

This is your focus holding the peaceful feelings of the beautiful desert island and playing your game in this relaxed calm state of mind. This will be holding you in or very close to the 'high zone' and if you can stay detached from whatever happens during your game and hold this feeling you will hit amazing shots. You are not attached to the outcome of how your golf goes this is the secret.

You could put a yellow dot on your golf glove, so that every time you set up you see it and this reminds you of the sun a **'shining ball of yellow'** *and the warm feeling the rays of sunlight give you as you feel them on your face, the back of your neck and your hands.* This helps to click you into the warm feelings of serenity and peace of the desert island, this is your trigger. You are giving your conscious mind a focal point so that you can allow your subconscious mind to take over and play your round through you.

You are thinking of the tranquil beach and the warm rays of sunlight while you barley concentrate on your round. This is how you drive your car everyday; you subconscious generally does the driving, while you are using your conscious mind to think about this and that.

How many times have you arrived at your destination and thought to yourself 'I don't remember driving here'. You can do it when driving so all you have to do is train yourself to do it when playing golf. This is similar to the 'driftwood' technique and puts you in the 'high zone' of peak performance by creating the right high vibrational feelings within you.

Remember if you hit a poor shot and get drawn into anger, frustration and disappointment you will be plummeting down from the 'high zone'. Practice this technique until you master it and your golf will improve as you learn how to hold yourself in the higher vibrations.

All you are putting your conscious mind on is the beautiful feelings of the tranquil peaceful desert island and the warm rays of sunlight. This is your dominant focus for your entire round and nothing that happens during your game can drag you away from that sense of serenity. Keep feeling the warm glow and you will be staying in the higher vibrations.

It's a great way to hold yourself in the 'high zone' and just allow the golf to unfold. This is the key play your round without giving it too much thought or energy put your focus on staying detached and at peace.

This technique can help train you to hold yourself in the correct mindset so that you can keep the negative energy at bay. You

'The mind game finally explained'

can even use a yellow golf ball and see that as the sun and your trigger to induce the warm serene feelings.

Eventually with practice your subconscious mind will automatically shift to the feelings of the desert island and the warm rays of sunlight when you look at the yellow dot or yellow golf ball etc and this is the goal, to naturally slip into the high zone when the trigger is engaged.

Chapter 10

Module 6

"Putts get real difficult the day they hand out the money."

-Lee Trevino-

Lee Buck Trevino is a retired American professional golfer regarded as one of the greatest players in professional golf history, and the greatest Hispanic golfer of all time

Visualisation

Brain Science

Let's first take a brief look at what brain science tells us about how our brain works; this will help you understand why visualisation can be so beneficial.

Visualisation is an excellent tool that you can use, which will have a direct influence on your subconscious mind. It will help create new thinking pathways within your brain that with repetition will change your programming and help let go of your inner resistance. When you visualise, you are in fact generating electrical impulses within your brain that fire down neural pathways and the more you repeat this, the more permanent and entrenched those pathways become.

In time these new pathways will become your new habitual way of thinking. In other words it becomes natural to think this way instead of the old more negative way. Once you have opened them up it then becomes natural to repeat this type of thinking because you have already forged the pathways. Do it enough and this becomes your instinctive way of thinking and feeling, the old habitual pathways will then without use close up.

Most of your instinctive negative responses to events in life are because you have been taught to think negatively about things, you have been programmed and this programming has become so engrained you just react in that way. You have no control over it, it just happens. This has left you with a multitude of habitual negative automatic reactions to whatever is going on, which simply recharges your inner resistance solidifying its power.

'A brown envelope from the tax office lands on the carpet you get a **sinking feeling** in your solar plexus, a negative gut reaction'.

'Somebody cuts you off at the traffic lights; you feel a surge of **anger** and **frustration**'.

'You miss a three foot putt, you feel **disappointed** and **anxious**'.

'You slice your drive, you feel **depressed** and **despondent**'.

All of these natural reactions are you feeling your energy vibration dropping. It's an awful feeling and it pulls you down the vibrational scale away from the higher vibrations and away from the 'high zone'.

These negative automatic reactions have happened so often in your life that they have carved deep neural pathways within your brain. The more you experience these reactions the more solidified the neural pathways become. It's like water running down a mountain, it eventually carves its way into the rock and this becomes the route it always travels.

You end up with thousands of permanent neural pathways open within your brain just waiting for the same situation to pop up again. You are a human being that is going through everyday of your life acting like a robot automatically reacting to the electrical firings within your brain. And most of the time it's your inner resistance that has created these neural pathways locking you into negative thoughts and feelings, which simply feed it.

And every time it happens you just get the negative feelings, you haven't got time to think about it, it just happens. This is your programming kicking in and it's all controlled by your subconscious mind.

Visualisation is a great tool to change all of that and create new positive habitual reactions, so that you don't hundreds of times a day plunge down in vibration. In fact you can create positive automatic reactions so that you jump up in vibration instead. Your subconscious mind is controlling the vast majority of the feelings you experience everyday and it's all based on the programming that you predominantly downloaded in the first six years of your life.

Now that wouldn't be so bad if you were programmed with

mainly positive input but unfortunately very few of us have been that lucky. It seems the world is geared up at this point in our evolution to bombard us with negative energy. Just look at the media, television and newspapers all doom and gloom it's everywhere around us.

Getting this negative impulse stuff out of your mind especially during your round of golf is imperative to ensure you maintain your vibration at the highest possible level. Managing your vibration is what it's all about.

Visualisation is a tool that will help you change your instinctive reactions and weaken your inner resistance, naturally keeping you at a higher vibrational level in the process.

Golf

Visualising your round of golf and picturing yourself lift the trophy at the end of the tournament before you play, is a powerful way of creating that very thing. Here is a true story of somebody who used visualisation over a period of time and it manifested astonishing results.

Major James Nesmith was an average golfer shooting in the mid to low nineties. Then during the Viet Nam war he was taken prisoner and spent seven years in solitary confinement. For the period of his incarceration he spoke to no one and had no physical exercise. To keep himself sane he devised a visualisation game, he would play a round of golf every day, using his imagination to make the game as real as possible.

He would see himself on his home town course and he tried to fully experience every aspect of the game. The warm sun on the back of his neck as he bent over his shot, the smell of the fresh cut grass and the feel of the light breeze on his face. The joy of sinking a long putt and the feeling of satisfaction, as he completed a fine round of golf.

He savoured every shot as if it were real and took as long as it would take to play a real round of golf. He did this everyday to help him through the terrible hardships he was going through.

Eventually he was released and an astonishing thing had taken place, the first time he set foot on a golf course he shot a 74, he had cut 20 strokes off his average and that's without swinging a club for seven years. How could this possibly happen you may wonder? The answer is quite simple; 'He believed he could do it'. The constant visualisation had programmed his subconscious mind to believe that he could play to that level; he had carved new neural pathways within his brain, more positive neural pathways in respect of his abilities on the golf course.

You see the subconscious mind as powerful as it is cannot tell the difference between a real round of golf and an imagined one. The more you impress your mind with positive images about something the more the subconscious will come to accept it. Then eventually a reprogramming will occur and the old programming of 'what was possible' will be replaced with the new one.

Once the subconscious accepts it, this is what you will get. Suddenly you are a top class golfer without even swinging a club. You can apply visualisation to any aspect of your game, driving, iron play, short game or putting. The more you imagine yourself as brilliant the better you will be. Most golfers will have experienced this to some degree at some time during their career. I remember one time for some inexplicable reason I thought I was brilliant at getting out of bunkers; I even used to aim for them. I really liked being in a bunker and I always played a brilliant shot. I think this occurred because of one brilliant bunker shot that I managed to pull off.

This confidence faded after a time and I was back to my usual hopeless level of bunker play but for a while I had somehow developed a strong belief that I was good at bunker shots and as long as I held that belief and felt the confidence, I was good but when the doubts crept back in my vibration dropped accordingly (in respect of bunker shots) and my temporary ability slipped away. I hadn't put any practice in but I had by pure fluke somehow attained the belief that I was good.

This happened again a few years ago, I am an eighteen handicap and decided I wanted to be a seven handicap. I tried to believe I was a seven and over two days I played twenty-seven holes of golf and when I played I remember feeling that I was a seven handicap, I really made an effort to gently but truly feel and believe it. After I had played I looked at my scorecards and I had dropped eleven shots, averaging out at a seven handicap. Then when I stopped visualising I drifted back to my old thinking and beliefs and next thing you know I was playing to an eighteen handicap again.

The secret of getting the most from your visualisation is not to will something into being with focused will power and concentration with a mindset of wanting it to happen but to see it as having already happened. You are not willing the ball into the hole as it fly's through the air and rolls over the contours of the green, you are experiencing the joyous feelings that it has already dropped into the hole. You **know** it has already dropped into the hole.

This feeling of certainty is what you are looking for and with practice you will be able to generate it at will. To feel and believe it has already happened, you have to feel the emotions and joy that you would experience after you have played the perfect shot and you do this before you even hit the ball. The more powerfully you can do this, the more energy you are giving to actually creating it. It's all about belief, we live in a belief driven universe and with belief you can achieve anything.

During your round trying to impose your will on making the ball go in the hole will of course help because this pushes away any doubts that might be trying to get your attention but the best result is obtained by **'feeling'** that it has already dropped into the hole. It's the feelings of success that generate the result not so much the thoughts. Your true power to create is generated through your feelings. The more you practice visualising and generating the **'feelings'** the better you will get, it's no different to learning to swing a golf club, practice makes perfect.

I once heard a comment by Johnny Miller in respect of Tiger's amazing ability to land the big putts; he said **'Tiger's father taught him that if he really believed, he could make things happen'**. This sums it up, Tiger has incredible belief that things will happen for him on the golf course and of course more often than not they do. This ability to believe was instilled there by his father at a very young age and Tiger readily took it all on board.

His ability to really believe he can land the big shots is subject to less doubts than everybody else, so he makes more of them. He has less negativity getting in the way. In other words he has less heavy negative energy in respect of golf (less inner resistance) trying to pull down his vibration so he stays closer to the 'high zone' and he does this naturally, that's why he is the best.

Tiger was a golf prodigy from the age of three when he actually beat Bob Hope on a TV show in a putting contest. This indicates that his father's positive influence was instilling in him in the first vitally important six years the belief that he was an amazing golfer. This positive early years programming is I feel one of the main reasons he has been such a force in golf.

Feel it

Truly believing you can land the shot or win the tournament is more a case of creating the correct feelings within you, the feelings of already having done it. It's you that must change and when you change what's going on inside of you, your reality changes accordingly.

You must believe that you have made the shot; you must believe that you have won the tournament. This is the secret and this will help keep the doubts at bay and hold you in the 'higher vibrations' where you can more easily attain the 'high zone' where success flows naturally to you.

Using visualisation before and during your round of golf is important but you should also use it to see yourself next month, next year or five years from now. Picture the future in any way that you desire, slipping on the Masters Green Jacket at Augusta, lifting the Claret Jug, achieving the World's number one spot or even winning your club stableford.

As well as moving into your fabulous new house, buying yourself a new Ferrari and looking after your family financially. You are creating your future now, so you should have definite targets to aim for. Not having targets encourages an unfocussed mindset that is heading you towards exactly that, an unfocussed future.

When you prepare to hit your drive off the tee you don't think I will hopefully hit it somewhere down the fairway, you pick a specific target to aim for. The same applies to your life, get focused and use visualisation to steer it exactly where you want it to go.

Then you must be ever vigilant always holding your vision and doing your visualisation every day. The moment you relax your old unfocussed mentality will drift back in and your inner resistance will take back over, pushing negative pictures into your mind to encourage negative thoughts and feelings resulting in poor results.

As long as you have inner resistance it will always be waiting in the wings to infect your thought patterns in order to generate the negative feelings within you that it is after.

Routine

Develop a routine before each round of golf to enable you to visualise how you want the day to go. I find a relaxing bath with couple of candles burning creates a great environment to practice my pre-day visualisation. You can use any method you prefer to get you in a comfortable relaxed state of mind, maybe you like to go for a quiet walk in nature to attain the right mindset. Remember you are going to visualise your success and set the serene mood for the day at the same time.

Just get comfortable and spend maybe 10-15 mins visualising the coming round of golf. See it as vividly as possible and try to experience the feelings as if it has already happened. See the look on your caddies face when you card a 61 and the joyous energy that this creates. Your subconscious doesn't know the difference between what's imagined and what's real so this is the purpose of this exercise. You are convincing your subconscious mind that the game has already been played and you have had a brilliant round of golf.

If your subconscious accepts your visualisation then that is what you will get. You are capable of incredible things when you can harness the power of your subconscious mind and get it to help you, rather than leaving it to devote its energy to monitoring that you stay in your comfort zone. You can literally produce your greatest round of golf every time you step on to the golf course, if you really believe you can and convincing your subconscious mind is the way to achieving this. Visualising your round is an extremely powerful tool to have in your box.

I am not suggesting you spend four hours going through every shot but what I am advising is that you spend 10-15 minutes in a relaxed state seeing some of your shots but more importantly creating the feelings of success. You can visualise each shot when you are on the course just before you play it and again it's the feelings you are looking to experience. You are trying to 'believe', that's your goal 'believe'. It's all about that and the more you practice visualising to make yourself really 'believe' the better you will play.

Doing the driftwood meditation first for 15 minutes then going straight into your pre-round visualisation for 15 minutes would be a great way to attain the right mindset and generate the correct feelings. This would get you into 'the high vibrational zone' and set your beliefs for the day. Practice all of the time believing you can do something and visualisation is the way you can do this. If you believe it, you can achieve it.

Another good method for generating belief is to write things down as if they have already happened. You could before your round take a pen and paper and write something like the following:

'I have played a brilliant round of golf. I am so ecstatic that I have played so well and carded a 61. Everything went brilliantly for me today, I got the luck of the bounce and every putt went in. My swing felt natural and fluent; when I struck the ball it was sweet and pure. I felt so relaxed and serene on the course.

My driving was outstanding, I hit every fairway and my approach shots were perfect. I was able to place the ball on any spot that I wanted and I felt truly tranquil and in the high zone. I felt so happy and calm and it was one of the most enjoyable and best rounds of golf I have ever played'.

Of course shooting a 61 is more believable for a professional than an amateur, so set your targets to suit you. Maybe five or six shots better than your handicap to start with this will be more acceptable and give your inner resistance less opportunity to generate doubts. You can keep changing the target as you progress.

You can write anything you want and the idea is to imagine you have played the perfect round and get into the 'feeling' zone of having done that. It's the feelings that the subconscious mind really pays attention to and absorbs. The feelings are all important, feelings convince the subconscious and when the subconscious accepts it you truly believe it and then it happens.

Remember it's your inner resistance that you have to overcome and that is what is negatively influencing your subconscious mind, so convincing your subconscious is a very important step. Feelings are the language that your subconscious mind understands and this can help you get rid of the negative influence of your inner resistance.

Feelings are vibrational energy; thoughts can be weak and meaningless without the injection of feelings. It's all about vibration; you see your inner resistance is more like a collection of negative vibrations that have took up residence within you and this drags you down to a level that your subconscious has come to regard as home.

This 'home' or 'comfort zone' is where your subconscious wants to keep you, that is what it is programmed to do, ensure that you as a vibrational being stay within the vibrational frequency range that is regarded as normal for you. Thoughts won't break you out of it but powerful feelings will. High vibrational feelings will help infuse your energy field with new energy and that will lift you out of your programmed comfort zone.

Thoughts without feelings have little vibrational energy, they are powered by the feelings that you put with them. It's the feelings that carry the real power.

When you rise up everything gets better, you move into a frequency range where there is less of the negative stuff. Fear, doubt, anxiety, worry and frustration struggle to survive in the higher vibrational zones they cannot exist there. So you experience less of these types of low vibrational thoughts and feelings.

Visualisation is a tool you can use to help get you up in frequency closer to or into the 'high zone' so that you can play at a higher level. As you play your round you are looking to hold the feelings of success, the feelings of playing a fantastic game of golf. This is what you must keep going back to, the way you felt during your visualisation. Feel it and it will happen.

Used correctly visualisation is one of the most powerful tools you can use to alter your vibrational frequency and reprogram your comfort zones. Mastering this skill will be a tremendous addition to your tool box and as always remember practice makes perfect.

Chapter 11

Module 7

"Of all the hazards, fear is the worst."

-Sam Snead-

Samuel Jackson Snead was an American professional golfer who was one of the top players in the world for most of four decades

Inner Lake

This module is about stilling your inner energy. It will calm you down and step aside from any negative energy that is circulating and put you into the 'high zone' using a simple technique. This can be done as you are taking each shot and when mastered you will be able to build it into your routine without anybody even noticing what you are doing. It is incredibly effective and when perfected it is all you will need to get yourself into the correct mindset and feeling place for every shot.

This can also be used if you are not playing well to get your game back on track. It will take your mind off what is going wrong and allow you to have a simple focus to concentrate on. You can steady the ship by following these principles, keeping you in contention no matter what has gone before. This technique can really turn your game around even when you are having a bad day.

It is another way to get your vibration up when needed and simple enough to use and an effective tool for every golfer to have in his bag. However it is also all you need to tap into peak performance, so do not underestimate the power of this technique. If this is comfortable for you to use then it is all you need to get yourself into the 'high zone' of peak performance.

Every bad shot during a game of golf is due to negative energy creeping in somewhere. Keep the negative energy out and you will play at your very best every time, staying in the 'high zone' is the trick and to do that you must train your mind to be able to take you there whenever you want. This technique will help you to train your mind and with repetitive practice become second nature.

Unplug

A quick and effective way to up your game is to unplug yourself from your conscious mind. You step aside from thinking about and analysing your game through your conscious mind and allow your subconscious mind to take over. Now I am not talking about the subconscious mind that wants to stick to the early years programming, I am talking about leaving that behind too and allowing your subconscious to play the shot for you unhindered by your early years programming free from the influence of your inner resistance.

You have to simultaneously step aside from your conscious mind and your early years programming and let your subconscious mind take over unhindered by your inner resistance. And you do that by settling the energies and getting into the 'high zone', above the vibration of your inner resistance, this is how you can achieve peak form every time you play.

I previously said your subconscious mind 'plays the shot for you' because that's what it feels like. You almost step out of the way mentally and another power takes over. Of course you physically swing the club and you hit the ball but from a conscious awareness point of view, you are barely paying attention. I have employed this method and hit shots I know I did not normally have the talent or ability to carry off.

My golf prowess is only average and I am just a social player but when I successfully employ this technique I can play far beyond my normal level. I have never put in the practice and that is reflected in my average scores but when using this method I have played to around 12 to 16 shots better than my physically attained level.

For a professional golfer that means you can hit scores probably at least 3 or 5 shots better than your average. And that makes all the difference between success and failure. And more importantly when you are having a struggling round this technique will enable you to get your game back, ensuring that you drop a lot less shots than you might have.

Let me explain exactly how it feels when you use this technique. Normally I don't like hitting a three wood off the fairway; it's a shot that I very rarely pull off with a great degree of success. I didn't even realise that when I went to play the shot and reached into my bag for the three wood there was a slight feeling of tension and reticence. In fact these barley perceptible ripples of negative energy just beneath the surface were there most of the time with just about every shot I played when I was using my normal thinking everyday conscious mind.

This is how we all feel everyday of our lives when we are thinking, watching and analysing life through our conscious mind. Hovering just beneath the surface there is always a constant mild vibration of tension, faint reverberations of negativity bubbling just beneath our conscious awareness (this is of course our inner resistance). We have become so used to this negativity tainted state of mind that we don't even realise it's there; it has become 'normal'.

It was only when I experienced the peace and tranquility of stepping aside from the conscious mind that I realised that something felt very different, the constant mild simmering tension had gone. I was experiencing life without the influence of my inner resistance probably for the first time.

In this calm, serene, tranquil state of mind you leave behind all the negative energy lodged within your inner resistance and gently rise above the negativity. You are still thinking through your conscious mind but your focus is not on golf, you are basking in peace and serenity and going with the flow, this is what you are thinking and feeling, this is what your conscious mind is focused on.

You are playing golf but you are concentrating on peace and serenity, the golf is something you are doing almost to one side through a haze of calm tranquil energies. You are not giving too much thought to your golf, certainly not the intense concentrated focus you would normally apply. You are aware you are playing but it's not the important thing that is going on in your mind.

When I attained this state of mind and reached into my bag for my three wood there were none of the usual faint ripples of negative energy disturbing my inner peace. I felt comfortable and relaxed, as I pulled the club from the bag and I knew something was different. I felt a relaxed sense of confidence, I knew it didn't matter which club I used, I would hit it well. I was devoid of doubts and the doubts were replaced with a feeling of certainty. I guess this is how you feel when your inner resistance is not part of you and exerting its negative influence.

I hit the three wood 235 yards onto the green six feet from the pin, my finest ever shot with that club. And the strange thing was I hardly put any effort into it, it all felt so relaxed and effortless, I couldn't believe the distance the ball had traveled. It felt like I had hit it about 120 yards not 235 yards. The usual energy sapping powerful swing full of effort and vigor was replaced with a nice easy smooth swing.

Next I used my driver and casually glanced down the fairway picking out an approximate target to aim at keeping away from the rough on the left hand side. I gave it no more thought, no working out distances and scrutinising my aim, no lining up the shot and pondering how the ball might roll on the fairway. I did none of these things instead I focused on holding my peaceful tranquil mindset and gently swung the club. It was easy and stress free and again it felt like I used no real power, strength or effort.

The ball flew off the tee and was dead on course for the right hand side of the fairway straight as an arrow. Pleased with my drive I set off down the fairway and to my amazement the ball had somehow worked its way across the fairway to the left hand edge of the fairway. The distance was ridiculous probably my longest ever drive around 300 yards and I could not see how the ball had curved to the left across to the other side of the fairway, no raised banks to roll off and the ball had flew perfectly straight. Again it felt like I had hit it with enough power to go around 150 yards certainly not the 300 yards it did go.

When I got to the ball I realised that the pin was tucked into the back right hand corner of the green and had my ball stayed out right I would have faced a very difficult approach shot. As it happened I was now on the left hand side of the fairway and in the perfect position for my approach shot with the full green opened up. From the tee I could not see the pin position so had no idea what the best side of the fairway would be. In fact even if I had known I would have just been happy to be on the fairway let alone be able to choose which side I wanted the ball to end up on.

Now this happened again and again my tee shot somehow without my input getting itself into the perfect position even though I did not know the pin position. This is how incredible your subconscious mind is when it is freed up from your inner resistance and you are in the 'high zone'. If you can learn this technique and play your golf in the 'high zone' through your subconscious mind you will literally astound yourself.

This is the key to peak performance. How many of the worlds top professionals have we seen allow tension to creep into their mind during the final eighteen holes of a major tournament and suddenly let it all slip away. Their vibration has been dragged down by negative energy sneaking into their mind and their form deserts them.

The trick is to hold serenity and inner peace no matter what and nothing else should be on your mind. Steve Davies the snooker player explained it well when he said *'when it really does matter, you have to play as if it doesn't matter'*. This describes the correct mindset; you must be serene and hold your inner peace not really thinking about your game just focused on tranquility and inner peace.

Thinking it matters allows tension and stress into the equation, it opens the door for your inner resistance to get to work. Then you get flooded with ridiculous thoughts 'what if I mess up', 'what if I win', what if I look silly' etc. This is how your inner resistance blows it in for you and this is what it wants, to keep you in a state of negativity and away from success. Keep it quiet by training yourself to hold the feelings of serenity and inner peace in your mind.

"I have never felt so serene on a golf course"

After taking the lead in the British Open 2009

-Tom Watson-

American professional golfer one of the all time greats winner of eight majors.

The 'Inner Lake' Technique

Every time you set up to the ball you are looking to slip into the feelings of serenity and inner peace, this is called the 'Inner Lake'. This is all that matters and with practice you can perfect this technique, which creates the correct mindset to consistently play golf at your very best, this puts you in the 'high zone' for every shot.

If you can imagine inside of your chest down to your stomach there is an 'inner lake' and this lake is perfectly still, no ripples on the surface or currents beneath the surface, just perfectly still. The top of the lake is as still as the deepest part of the lake. This is how you can picture your 'inner peace'. Holding the feeling of a still inner lake is the trick and not allowing negative energy in to create any disturbance.

1. Set up for your shot casually picking your spot and taking aim trusting that your subconscious will know exactly where to hit the ball. Don't think too much about the shot, a quick visualisation of the ball in flight and the end result is enough to instruct your subconscious of what you want.

2. As you stand over the ball take a deep breath or two and feel the still calm feeling in the area of your solar plexus, as your 'inner lake' becomes perfectly still. Sense the inner peace that this creates and bask in that feeling. This is all you should be thinking about, forget golf at this point just holding the feeling of the still inner lake is the secret and it's all about the feelings of peace that this image gives you. (At this point even if you can't fully settle the lake down and there is a couple of ripples on the surface don't worry because that doesn't matter as long as you can 'feel' the stillness, this is the key the still feeling within).

3. As you hold the feeling of stillness within, you may feel your fingers releasing their grip on the club to the point of no grip to speak of, the club is just gently resting in your hands. Your fingers may even open up slightly barely touching the grip. Or you may just have the sense of feeling totally calm and relaxed, now you are in the right place mentally to play your shot. Your conscious mind is fully occupied with the correct feelings this is when you are ready to swing the club.

4. Now you swing the club, it should feel easy and effortless no thought of power and effort, just free loose and easy, stay focused on holding the feeling of inner peace and serenity, keep that 'inner lake' still. You should be so deep in the correct feeling place and seeing that inner lake still that you are hardly even aware of swinging the club, it just happens as you concentrate on peace and tranquility. No thinking of the shot at this point just bask in the high vibrational energies of serenity, inner peace and stillness and let the shot go. It's all about holding the inner feelings of peace as the shot takes place. You have no real concern of where the ball is going, just a sense that it is on the line you have chosen, your only thoughts are basking in the peaceful energies.

Keep practicing this technique and you will train yourself to be able to tap into the most powerful mindset from which to play your golf. You are capable of achieving anything in the correct mindset and this is a brilliant and simple technique to put yourself into the 'high zone'. You can practice this anytime anywhere it doesn't have to be on the golf course. I do this many times during the day and this makes it easier for me to reproduce it on the golf course. This is just as important as practicing hitting golf balls if not more important.

I often take myself to the feeling of inner peace in my solar plexus and try to hold that lake still. I find this little visualisation extremely beneficial when negative energy has crept into my mind and caused disturbance to my 'inner lake'. This centres your energy and focuses you on serenity and inner peace, which lets go of any negative energy that maybe circulating in your mind or trying to grasp your attention.

The more you do this during your day the more skilled you will be at recreating the feeling. It's just the same as training yourself to do anything else, practice makes perfect. And it helps you to release day to day negativity allowing your life to run more smoothly in the process.

Had Rory McIlroy been aware of this technique I am certain that his final round at the 2011 US Masters would have had a very different outcome. It seems to me this was a classic case of negative energy creeping in and dragging down his vibration a fraction into a slightly lower zone, where it was difficult for him to play golf to his normal level.

'The mind game finally explained'

I believe his inner peace was disturbed, as the negative energy caught his attention pulling down his vibration. His conscious mind was tussling with negative energy, which he could have 'mind managed' had he practiced the principles of this technique. This meant he was not holding the feeling of inner peace in his solar plexus but was caught up in the drama of events unfolding on the golf course.

Of course that is perfectly understandable a young man leading one of the biggest tournaments in the world going into the last day. It's no surprise that tension, anxiety and apprehension may have reared their ugly head disturbing his inner peace in the process and messing with his form. I am certain Rory will win many Majors in his career he is one of the most talented golfers we have ever seen but I am equally certain he will win more if he learns how to keep that 'inner lake' still when needed.

Mind management is so important on the golf course and without understanding how it all works through high vibrational thinking and employing some simple usable techniques to get you as an energy body into the 'high zone' you are relying solely on your ability to swing a golf club. And this means you are limited in what you can achieve because your mind will very rarely be in the right place. Golf more than probably any other sport is mind focused and every serious player must train their mind as well as their body if they are to have any chance of realising their true potential. Without mind management techniques you will occasionally hit the 'high zone' but I doubt that it will be when it really matters and it won't be that often.

By pure chance circumstances will sometimes come together allowing your vibration to rise and your golf to hit top form. Now with these techniques available and knowledge of what's going on through HVT you can train yourself to be in the 'high zone' most of the time and when your mind drifts you will know how to get it back. And you will know when you are slipping out of the high zone.

The difference between the greatest players and the rest up until now has in most cases been their level of self-belief because this eliminated many of the doubts which would have pulled down their vibration. This helped them stay in the higher vibrational zones more than the rest. Belief eliminates doubt, which is negative energy, allowing your vibration to rise. Strong self-belief meant less of an influence from heavy slow vibrational negative energy (doubts).

Most players are battling themselves more than the golf courses that they are playing and this is why they never achieve what they could. They think the course and their opponents are the competition, when the real battle is within their own mind. I have no doubt that the world's finest golfers when perfecting techniques to attain the 'high zone' will soon be hitting scores beyond our belief. Rounds in the fifties will soon be commonplace, as the worlds elite golfers learn to bring their mind game up to par with their physical game and god given natural talent.

The analogy of the inner lake is one of my favourites to create the inner stillness but you could easily make up you own method to achieve this such as stilling a white feather gently blowing in the breeze or calming the leaves of a great oak tree shimmering in the wind or maybe settling the flame of a candle flickering etc. So why not use your imagination and create your own version if this better suits you and remember it's all about the feelings of peace within. This is the key, find that feeling of serene peace within and focus on that.

'The mind game finally explained'

Chapter 12

Module 8

"If you worry about making bogeys, it makes the game that much more difficult. You put more pressure on yourself without even noticing it. It makes a difference to take it easy when things aren't going right."

-Sergio Garcia-

New Perspective

Forming a new perspective is another great way to shift old beliefs. Standing back and looking at something in a slightly different way can be very empowering. Often we get so fixed in our ideas that we forget you can alter the way that you see things and when you do this a new feeling arises in respect of what we are looking at. A new emotional avenue is opened allowing a change in thinking and feeling to take place. It is very liberating to realise that things don't always have to be viewed as we are told they are.

In respect of your round of golf this is done by looking at par differently to everybody else. Take one shot off each hole and that becomes your new par. So you are looking at a par three as a two, par four as a three and a par five as a four. This creates a new paradigm for you, which will begin changing your old beliefs and expectations.

This generates real tangible goals that will soon become engrained within your new perspective. Shooting for three on a regular par four and expecting to achieve it is your aim. You are not to take risks but to play within yourself and still expect to achieve your 'new' par on every hole. A well placed drive followed by an accurate approach shot is the route to take. Leaving you always with a putt for your 'new' par and two shots for an old par.

The trick is to train your mind to think in a new way on the golf course. The more you can accept this new perspective the more your beliefs will grow. Expect to shoot 18 under for every round that you play and you will soon be hitting scores way below your old expectations. You are not to be limited by the thinking of others, let them see a par four as acceptable and a birdie three as a great result but to you a three is acceptable and a two a great result.

Changing your expectations is the key, the more you look at each hole in this new way the more you will ingrain that new view within your mind. You are breaking free from old paradigms and constant repetition will forge new neural pathways in your brain. As you know when you have a thought an electrical pulse fires in your brain down a specific pathway, then every time you have that thought the same pathway fires. This creates habitual thinking pathways and we are going to create new habitual thinking pathways so that expecting a three on a par four becomes as natural to you as the old way of thinking.

Repetition is the key here and soon you will believe and expect to hit one under par for every hole. Simply practice thinking this way every time you set foot on the golf course and you will be amazed at how it all begins to look and feel different. Changing your beliefs is the secret and this exercise is a great way to achieve that.

Every time you stand on the tee think **'three'** (on a par four) look down the fairway and really feel that this hole is a **'three'**. Imagine your drive landing in the perfect place for your approach shot. See your approach shot landing right on the pin leaving you a relatively simple four or five foot putt. Your practice is to generate the feelings that this hole is a **'three'** and making yourself believe that it is. You are going for **'three'**, you are planning for a **'three'**, you are picturing a **'three'**, you are expecting a **'three',** you believe that you will comfortably get a **'three'**.

You are not playing for a four and hoping you might get a three, you are playing for a three and hoping you might get a two. You are focused on a **'three'** to you this is par it doesn't matter what everybody else thinks. It's all about practicing the feelings; this is what is forging those new neural pathways in your brain. The more powerful the feelings the more ingrained the pathways become. The more ingrained, the more you believe. The more you believe, the more times you will score a **'three'**.

Remember you can do anything if you believe it; it's all in your mind. You really can shoot one under for every hole if you can make yourself believe you can. Belief is the key, harness this power through repetitive practice and you can achieve anything. This exercise is about forging those new beliefs. And as you see each hole in a new light you will be keeping out the influence of your inner resistance because you have your mind occupied with positive thoughts and feelings.

Roger Bannister would never have broken the four minute mile if he had listened to the limitations of others; he dared to believe the impossible could be done. He looked at things differently to everybody else and the rest is history. They told him it was impossible for a man to run a mile in under four minutes, it was a physical impossibility for a human. He didn't listen to their limitations; he believed it could be done. Within weeks of him breaking four minutes three other runners broke through the barrier. They were held back by what they believed, he showed them the way. You too can push back the barriers, you just have to train yourself to expect something different and ultimately to believe something different.

If you don't train your mind to believe you can achieve better scores you are keeping yourself to the old limitations, the limitations of others. Your practice and natural ability can only take you to a certain level, then you hit 'what is possible' imposed by the achievements and thinking of others.

This is where you can get stuck in the pack, with all the other golfers. To break free from the pack and smash down the barriers you have to dare to think differently, you have to realise you can think differently.

You have to make yourself believe in a different perspective, a new way of looking at it. Then you will soon be breaking down the barriers and showing everybody else the way.

Energy Shift

Changing the way that you see things also shifts the energy balance. Expecting to shoot a three on a par four means you take out the wanting and hoping element. Wanting and hoping are another way you can let negative energy sneak into your mind. Expecting allows you more easily to hold your inner peace and serenity ensuring that you increase your chances of actually attaining a three. Striving for a three is not the way to achieve it, expecting it in a calm relaxed state of mind is the secret.

Any method that you can utilise to hold onto your serenity and inner peace is the way forward. This is the key to attaining new levels of performance, training your mind to expect something helps you to stay peaceful and serene. Not expecting but hoping or wanting can easily allow in tension and anxiety. Negative energy can be very subtle in the ways that it enters your mind and gently disturbs your inner peace. You may hardly notice the ripples of negativity, as it begins to generate waves of energy, just like a small pebble thrown into a still pond.

You may sense a slight tightening of the grip, a barley detectable tensing of the facial muscles, an ever so faint contraction of the shoulders or you may not even be able to detect the destructive energy until it's too late. Methods to focus your mind are essential to ensure that you stay in the 'high zone' and hold the feeling of serenity and inner peace and stay relaxed and tranquil. Maintaining your vibration at the highest level is what it is all about and being in control of your thoughts and feelings is paramount to ensure negativity is kept at bay. Serenity and inner peace is your barometer and if you can sense these feelings within, then you are holding yourself in the 'high zone'.

After you practice this 'new perspective' for a while you will find that you naturally do it without trying and this is what you are looking to achieve. You are retraining your mind to feel comfortable seeing things in a slightly different way. This is how you adjust what you believe and create new beliefs. Belief is the secret of this life and the true 'genie in the lamp' of this world, if you can really truly believe something then it will happen. You are much more powerful than you realise and harnessing the power of your subconscious mind is the key and to do that you just have to make yourself believe and let go of the old limiting beliefs.

The 'new perspective' method can be used in other ways on the golf course lets take putting for example. When you are faced with a forty-foot putt instead of hoping to take two shots but accepting that you might take three and being relatively happy with that, try to focus on feeling that you can achieve it in one and accepting the very real possibility of two. From now on you want to feel that you want it in one and expect it in one. If you really expect to sink it in one then this helps you to believe that you can do it and this removes any subtle waves of negative energy that might be sneaking into your mind.

Standing over your putt with an expectation of 'two would be great, but three is acceptable', is leaving that door ever so slightly open for negativity to slip in. Standing over your putt with an expectation of 'I will sink this in one' and generating the associated feelings is closing that door just a little bit more.

The same applies to little chip shots and bunker shots around the green; you expect them to go in. No more hoping to get them close, you want to see them dropping in the cup and this is what you intend when you set up for the shot. And remember never allow yourself to feel disappointed if they do miss.

It's all about your mind and learning to shift your thoughts a fraction here and a fraction there to access the correct feelings. You must become an expert at conjuring up the feelings of the high zone and basking in them, allow them to wash over you and become familiar with them. This is how you learn to hold the feeling place of the 'high zone' and that is what changes your beliefs.

The more you practice this the more you will see your ball dropping into the hole.

Belief is the key

The truth is, 'if you believe it, you will achieve it' and that means it is possible to go round a golf course in eighteen shots that's eighteen holes in one. You may feel it's not possible to hit a golf ball five hundred yards but that again is just your mind allowing its conditioning to believe in barriers. History is littered with people who have pushed back barriers and it will continue to happen in golf and its all about what you believe is possible. There are endless recorded cases of people doing 'impossible' things, a one hundred pound woman lifting a car off a trapped child for example:

A woman saved the life of a seven year old boy after she found the strength to free him from under a one-tone car and then gave him the kiss of life. She said 'The car was on top of Jean-Luc and I somehow managed to push it off him, I don't know where I found the strength, I think nature just takes over'.

http://www.breakingnews.ie/archives/2003/1125/world/woma

n-lifts-car-off-boy

Apparently it's not possible for her to do that but somehow she has done it and if a woman can really do that do you think a man can't hit a golf ball 500 yards? Of course he can but we just have to break free from our conditioning of what we have been told is possible and make ourselves believe. It is happening slowly over years at a crawling pace, a tiny fraction at a time, as we collectively, as the human race push back the barriers of belief in every area of our lives.

If a score of eighteen is the ultimate round of golf then it just shows you how far away we are from that peak level. Tiger Woods has come along and pushed back the boundaries, he has shown us more is possible and that has opened the door for others to believe. Just like Roger Banister, Tiger has done the impossible and in golf terms he has jolted us forward. His example has given us all a boost in our own self-belief of what we can achieve.

Sinking forty-foot putts is about belief and that's all you have to do, make yourself believe and that means have no doubts, that is what this technique is about, changing your perspective so that you have no doubts. You have practiced your golf swing to get your game to the level it is at today, now it is time to practice with your mind and really move things on. This method is about learning to think differently and using it when you step onto the golf course is how you practice it.

I know you have experienced standing over a thirty or forty-foot putt and knew that you were going to sink it. This has happened to every golfer at sometime, amateur and professional. Maybe it hasn't happened very often but it will have happened. On that day you have by chance fell into the mindset of believing without any doubts and when this happens a feeling of certainty comes over you.

This is the mindset that we are trying to train you to be able to generate at will. The 'new perspective approach' will help you practice getting into the right state of mind, the mindset of believing, the mindset of certainty.

As with anything the more you practice the better you will get and it's no different when retraining your mind. Again it's the feelings that really matter this is what you are practicing, generating the feelings of confidence and certainty.

The feelings forge the new neural pathways in your brain and with repetition they become permanent and habitual, they become your new beliefs. This is the key to a new thinking approach to your golf and a guaranteed way to achieve lower scores more consistently. As well as being a way to overcome your inner resistance and keep you in the 'high zone'.

Technique to attain the feelings

Having a simple technique to generate the feelings of certainty is the best way to practice the 'new perspective approach'. This should be used when you play every shot. Of course you can develop your own technique but for now I will explain to you one of my favourite methods.

Pick one of your all time favourite golfers and he/she is going to help you get into the feeling place of certainty. My favourite golfer is Seve Ballesteros and I enlist Seve's help when applying this technique.

I picture Seve talking to me as I am setting up for my tee shot. I accept that for me this hole (on a par four) is now a three and I softly picture how the hole will play. Nice drive, good approach shot and excellent putt.

Then I imagine Seve saying to me, *'you will make this shot, you just have to believe you can'*. He then says *'just relax and bask in your inner peace and serenity, all you need to focus on is holding your inner peace and serenity, don't think too much about the shot, just softly visualise it, I will help you'*. Then I picture the image of Seve aligning himself with my body and adding his energy and skill to mine, I almost feel like I am Seve.

Infused with the power of Seve Ballesteros I feel confident and sure I will hit a brilliant shot and I allow the feelings of certainty to gently pervade my mind. Still basking in serenity and inner peace I then play the shot, trusting that Seve will help me.

This may sound a little complicated for every shot but with practice you will soon polish this approach into a simple usable technique that powerfully achieves the objective. Feeling the presence of Seve is very reassuring and this helps eliminate doubts, keeping negative energy at bay. The fact that you have a little technique to focus on stops your mind from drifting and unknowingly allowing negative energy to sneak in. It's better to have something positive to think about at the crucial moment of playing your shot rather than having nothing particular in your mind.

Your focus should be on holding your serenity and inner peace and softly picturing your shot unfolding exactly as you want it. No 'intense willing', just a soft gentle picture of a brilliant shot. 'Intense willing' can be accompanied by tension, stress and anxiety all energies that you do not want in your mind, all negative and damaging to your vibration. A soft gentle picture does nothing to disturb the energies of peak performance, serenity and inner peace.

I also find it helpful watching DVD's of Seve playing, as this keeps him strong within my mind and easy to call on when I need him. I really feel his presence when I use this method and my belief level absolutely goes up with him on board. This new perspective technique and visualisation method to create the feelings of certainty is forging new neural pathways within my brain and the more I practice it, the more ingrained those pathways become. I am slowly teaching myself to believe that I can do something, I am learning to believe.

You may find that you prefer to use the method only during practice rounds and that's fine because once the neural pathways are opened up and used regularly you will automatically tap into them when you play your competition rounds. You will find after a while when you are faced with a one-hundred and sixty-yard approach shot that you actually believe that you will hit it close, you expect to hit it close and you will know with a feeling of certainty that you can do it. Whereas before you may have just hoped to hit the green. This is the change we are looking for, the belief level going up.

For a top professional you will be expecting and feeling with certainty that you will hit it to five-feet, rather than hoping and wanting five-feet but being happy with twelve to fifteen-feet.

Energy

On an energy level the technique is overriding old negative neural pathways of thinking and feeling and making new more positive neural pathways. This means you will be soon instinctively having the new feelings instead of the old ones. This keeps your energy vibration at the higher levels and you will be doing it naturally.

Resulting in more consistent golf at a higher level. It's all about changing your old thinking and feeling ways for new ones in order to permanently get your energy vibration up, this is the key to more success on the golf course and in every area of your life.

Holding the belief that you can make the shot and keeping your serenity and inner peace at all times is the goal. Utilising any methods that can help you do this will be beneficial to your game. You are now retraining your mind and gaining an in-depth understanding of how it works.

If you feel your serenity and inner peace slipping away you are slipping down in vibration, you are losing your form. You have somehow let negative energy in and it is dragging you down from the 'high zone'. Always use this as your barometer, become familiar with the feelings of serenity and inner peace. I can always tap into the correct feelings when I say to myself, **'thank you for helping me Seve, I know with your help I can make the shot',** this settles down the energies and gives me confidence.

Previously you have more than likely played your golf without any real control over your thoughts and feelings and still played to the level that you did. Your potential now to play at a consistently higher level is guaranteed.

All you have to do is begin using some of the mind training techniques that you are being taught. Build them into your routine and stick with your favorite methods; the ones that work for you and before long your golf will amaze even you.

Chapter 13

Module 9

"The mind messes up more shots than the body."

-Tommy Bolt-

Thomas Henry Bolt was an American professional golfer. Bolt was born in Haworth, Oklahoma. He served in the United States Army during World War II and turned professional in 1946

Logic Plan

The Logic Plan is a method used to systematically work your way around the golf course. This method utilises the conscious mind and focuses it on what needs to be done for each shot and each hole. This approach will help keep negative energy under control because you are occupying the conscious mind, especially now that you understand how it all works. This will help you to stay in a fairly high vibration for your round.

Many professional golfers use these types of methods very successfully even though they don't have the additional benefit of understanding it all through HVT.

As you are predominantly concentrating on a conscious mind approach you will still be playing at a level below your ultimate potential. Only when stepping aside from the conscious mind and playing through your subconscious mind unhindered by your inner resistance can you achieve your full potential in other words play fully in the 'high zone'. However the world's best are still mainly playing through their conscious mind and playing amazing golf, hitting scores in the sixties and low seventies on a regular basis.

Were they able to fully utilise their subconscious potential you would see golf on another level altogether.

I will explain to you how the logic plan approach works and why this method is so successful and how you can refine it slightly to stay closer to the high zone while using it.

Example

Lets presume you have parred the par five 505 yard second hole
at your home course many times, so why cant you do it every
time?

Let's answer the following questions:

1. Do you posses the ability to par or even birdie the hole?

2. Playing comfortably and easy can you reach the green in 3
shots?
(An easy 220 yard drive and two comfortable seven irons would
do it)

3. Can you hit an easy drive onto the fairway?

4. Can you hit an easy second shot onto the fairway?

5. Can you hit an easy approach shot onto the green?

6. Can you hole a reasonable length putt?

I would expect that you have answered yes to all of the above
questions, which shows it is within your capabilities to have a
good chance of a par or even a birdie. You can do it, so why don't
you do it every time? The answer is negative energy, when you let
doubts creep in you make mistakes. This is what creates bogeys,
double bogeys and worse.

By logically thinking about your game and working out what you
believe is possible to you, you eliminate doubts. You push doubts
from your thinking and give them less chance of arising, as you
play each hole. You create a believable plan of action that you
truly feel you are capable of carrying out.

You generate a focussed viewpoint that helps you keep your
concentration on your objective. The logic plan for each hole
gives you something to think about rather than having a less
concentrated focus, this helps stop negative thoughts randomly
arising. No plan leaves you at the mercy of your inner resistance,
a plan or indeed any of the modules helps keep your inner
resistance quiet and focuses your mind on the correct way to
feel.

Really it's all about belief because that is the key to absolutely anything, if you believe it, you can achieve it. The logic plan helps you to plan a series of shots that you believe you can execute. You are following a logical plan of action towards your goal. A plan that you believe you can achieve, something you feel is within your capabilities.

Standing on the tee of a par five is often daunting for an amateur golfer. The sheer distance creates tension, as you think you must hit the ball a long way to have any chance of reaching the green in three and this is what opens the door for negative energy to creep in. When the negativity gets hold of you and you sense it in your body as tension, worry or fear this is when you make mistakes. Having a sensible achievable plan helps take the tension out of it and keeps your vibration as high as possible.

For a professional golfer it's slightly different they are comfortable on the par fives and are thinking more about reaching the green in two and getting a birdie or an eagle. They are much more positive about what they can do and this firmly closes the door on negativity creeping in.

They know they can do it and this allows a professional to play golf with much less negative energy vying for their attention. Of course this can all change when they are in contention for a big win and that's when negativity can easily infect their mind, drag them down the vibrations and mess up their chances.

For a professional a logic plan helps them stay focussed during the big tournament and stops the mind from wandering. Remember if negative energy creeps in your vibration will be coming down and that makes it all the more difficult to stop more negative energy from invading your mind.

Once that door is open beware because you could find yourself so dragged down by negativity that errors become unavoidable. It's all about your energy vibration and a well thought out logic plan for your round of golf will do wonders to keep you in as high a zone as possible ensuring that you will play at a high level.

It would be prudent for a professional in contention going on to the back nine of a major tournament (or indeed anybody in any competition) to have a well thought out logic plan to finish his/her round. This will give them a steady focus and keep their mind on the job helping alleviate any negative energy from infecting their thinking. This applies even if they have been playing really well and in the high zone because the inner disturbance could erupt at any time. Hopefully they will be able to hold the feelings of the high zone and finish their round without needing to revert to a logic plan approach.

The logic plan approach can be adapted to any part of your game, driving, irons, short game and putting.

Driving:

You know what you are capable of with your driver. Maybe you can hit it fairly consistently down the fairway when you hit it 200 to 230 yards. An easy swing and smooth follow through gets you comfortably 200 to 230 yards. It's when you try for 280 yards that you put that extra power in and it can all go wrong.

The professional maybe finds he can comfortably hit it 270 to 280 yards with very little effort but when he goes for the big hit 320 yards plus it can be a little wayward.

Using your driver logically means playing within yourself slightly, which keeps the negativity at bay. Plan your round by aiming for what you know you are well capable of. You are looking to play relaxed golf and focussing on what you KNOW you can achieve.

Look at each hole and expect and plan to hit your drive a comfortable distance within your capabilities. No big risky shots. Nice relaxed shots with your focus on hitting the fairway. This is often referred to as percentage golf the difference now is you understand how your inner resistance works and how important it is for you to try to hold your vibration as high as possible.

This is percentage golf and mind management combined.

Irons:

Maybe you can hit a five iron 185 yards when you hit it well but lets plan it logically, you know you can hit your five iron 160 yards and that's playing within your power range. So for the 185 yards shot use your three iron or rescue club and hit it nice and easy.

Easy and smooth means less chance of negative energy creeping in.

You are looking to play shots that you KNOW you can pull off, not shots that you might pull off, wherever possible take the extra club and power down, this is the key. This will ensure that you are setting up to hit a shot that you feel you can execute, helping keep negative energy out of the equation.

Most amateur golfer are constantly playing shots that they are stretching for, which opens the door for negativity and can easily end in catastrophe. 'Going for it' is great when you pull the shot off but it is also a recipe for disaster because it opens the floodgates for negative energy.

Once you set up with the mentality to 'go for it' you have stepped onto a vibrational roller coaster ride. The energies will be going crazy and you will be putting yourself in an unsteady vibrational state where you have increased your chances of messing it up.

Playing the logical shot within your power range keeps the energies stable and gives you a far better chance of consistently achieving your goal.

Short Game:

You know what you are good at, stick with that and play the shots that you favour. This will keep it sensible and you will make fewer mistakes. I always like to use my nine iron around the green and that's because I have practiced with it and it now feels comfortable to me. I know the weight of the club and can more often than not, land the ball more or less exactly where I want to and this gives me confidence.

I play all kind of little chip shots with it and I know if I land the ball approximately one third of the way to the hole, it will roll on the last two thirds depending on gradient, surface etc.

If I use my wedge I don't have the same confidence and this is when mistakes can come in. The door to negative energy is slightly ajar when I set up to hit the wedge, so in my case it makes sense to always where possible to use the nine iron.

Playing your short game to a logic plan again means hit the shots you KNOW you can hit. No silly risks, look to play what you know you can play and do it in a relaxed state of mind. Once you pull out of your bag a club that does not keep you in this state of mind anything could go wrong. This is where you might scuff the ground, top it or get caught up in the grass.

Learn how to watch how you feel when you reach for a club, you should feel perfectly calm, serene and holding your inner peace. If you sense even the tiniest ripple of negative energy, then negativity has entered the equation.

It could result in a slight feeling of tension in your brow, tightness in your grip, an involuntary interruption in your breathing or a barley detectable wobble in your legs that indicates negative energy is present. Become an expert at sensing how your entire body feels so that you know when negative energy is affecting you.

Most of us are constantly in a state of negativity, a mild feeling of tension just beneath the surface. This has become our natural state of being through years of poor practice, now you have to change that if you are to reach your potential on the golf course.

This is why practicing feeling serene and holding your inner peace is so important, so that you can sense when you are not in that state of mind. When you know what the right state of mind feels like, you will know when you are not there. And when you are not there this means you are not in the 'zone' of peak performance and therefore playing below your very best. Negativity has seeped in and is dragging you down and even if it's only very slight it will have an affect.

The logic plan approach is all about having an organised plan so that you can stay in as high a zone as possible and keep the energies steady.

Putting:

I feel this is the area of the game that requires the most mind control. It is so easy when you are standing over a putt to let your mind slip into negative thinking. It's a relatively straight forward shot that requires the least effort physically but you have very little room for error and it is a minefield for doubts popping up. You have time to think as you play this shot and that is the danger. It's your thinking that can very easily become negative.

Your inner negativity or inner resistance will always be looking for an opportunity to influence you and it will put you off your putt if it can because its agenda is not the same as yours. You want to hole the putt and be successful, it wants you to miss the putt and feel the negative emotions generated. Disappointment, frustration and anger is what it's after because this recharges its battery. This is essential to its survival; this is what you are up against with every shot you play.

Incorporating a logic plan for putting is a great way to focus your attention and keep your inner negativity quiet. Your plan could be just expecting to get down in two putts and setting your stall out to achieve that. You could imagine a ten foot circle around the hole as you line up your first putt and concentrate on your ball getting into that circle. This will give you a very achievable target to aim for, which hopefully would leave you a sinkable four or five foot putt.

When you have achieved objective one getting into the ten foot circle you can focus on objective two, holing the putt. Imagine the hole sinking into the green slightly creating a three or four inch slope towards the hole giving you an eight inch target. See it as if it is really there and this will help you focus and increase your confidence, remember you just have to up your belief level to sink the putt, it's all about belief.

You need to feel that you can't miss now that you have a bigger target to aim at and this will help you feel confident and sure. Imagine the ball dropping into the hole and really try to enjoy the feelings of success that this generates. As the feelings of certainty wash over you make the putt.

Getting the best from a logic plan approach for your round is about giving your conscious mind a focus for every shot, which helps keep your inner negativity quiet. This will ensure the doubts are kept at bay and you can stay in as high a zone as possible. This doesn't stop you slipping into peace and serenity (the 'high zone') and believing you can hole the putt in one. It just means your logical approach is helping keep control of any negative energy that is floating around.

This is a method that has been used for many years and will undoubtedly help you concentrate and play at a higher level.

Until you master some of the other modules to get yourself into the 'high zone' following a logic plan for your round will undoubtedly improve your golf. And this will help train your mind to manage the negative energy making it easier for you to eventually move on to fully embracing the high zone and really tapping into the power of your unhindered subconscious mind.

The Technique

Draw up a logical plan of action for your round of golf. You are looking to play within yourself giving you a focus for every shot. I will show you how I would play the first hole of my home golf course Seaton Carew using a logic plan.

The first at Seaton is named 'The Rocket' a fairly straight forward 360 yard par 4. It's a straight hole with a pond to the right marked by out of bound white markers and the eighteenth runs adjacent to the left with sloping undulating rough between the two fairways. You don't want to end up in the rough, as your vision becomes impaired and you will more than likely be playing a blind shot. At around 280 yards the fairway dips and runs up between two very intimidating steep bunkers around twenty yards before the green.

The temptation is to go for it and try to reach the dip just before the green, which basically takes the two bunkers out of play. It looks reachable and indeed is but if you don't hit a good drive you could easily find yourself in a lot of trouble.

The logic plan approach for me would be to hit a three wood off the tee or even a rescue club sacrificing distance for accuracy. Bearing in mind this is the first hole it would be prudent to play an easy shot for the fairway rather than taking any risk before you are properly warmed up and of course this is ideal to set a smooth tempo for your round.

An easy relaxed tee shot on the first hopefully to around 200-220 yards and then my second shot would be a straight forward 140-160 yard approach shot. I would choose a five or six iron for this shot because I know I can hit it easy and still make the distance, rather than a full blooded (trying too hard) seven or eight iron.

Now if all has worked well I should be somewhere on the green with an outside chance of a birdie. My first putt would be to get the ball to stop in the imaginary ten foot circle around the hole leaving a reasonably simple four or five foot putt for par, if it drops in for a birdie all the better. If not then it's a visualisation of the hole being slightly sunken with sloping sides running down into it, giving me a nice big target to focus on helping me believe I will sink the putt. The trick is to have a focus point so your mind is concentrating and not wandering. A nice relaxed firm putt should get me off to a steady start with a par.

This is how you create a logic plan for your round. Analyse each hole and have a strategy to get the job done playing within your capabilities. Your scores will tumble and confidence will grow using this module. The more thought and planning you put into your logic plan for each hole the more you will actually believe you can achieve it. You will also when adopting this method be visualising each hole and each shot, again increasing your chances of achieving your goal and at the same time helping keep negative thoughts out of your mind, which will help keep your vibration up and closer to the 'high zone'.

Remember even if you are not able to click into the 'high zone' you are still better off trying to hold yourself up in as high a vibration as possible rather than slipping down into the lower vibrations.

This is a great way of learning to hold your focus and when you incorporate this method with high vibrational thinking you will maintain the highest possible vibration. It's no good using the logic plan method and still getting angry and frustrated, as this will simply counteract the good work you are doing.

You must use the method and be vigilant of your thoughts to ensure the best possible results.

Chapter 14

Module 10

"A leading difficulty with the average player is that he totally misunderstands what is meant by concentration. He may think he is concentrating hard when he is merely worrying."

-Bobby Jones-

Energy Out / Energy In

Our world of energy operates to a strict code of laws. The universal laws of energy say that whatever you give out, you will get back. And as you are actually made of energy, atoms, protons and neutrons you are in fact constantly pulsing out waves of energy into the universe, which are returning to you in like form. The energy that you pulse out is forever changing depending on your thoughts feelings and emotions.

Sometimes it may be very negative such as when you are angry, frustrated or disappointed and other times it may be positive such as when you are laughing, happy and successful.

The energy that you give out changes all of the time, as you go through different mood swings and encounter the different events and situations of your life. You may get some bad news and this makes you feel worried, upset, stressed or tense so at this time you are consumed by negative slow vibrational energy and that is what is going out from you into the universe. Another time you may have just booked a holiday or won a golf competition and this makes you feel happy, excited and joyful so this more high vibrational energy is what you are pulsing out into the universe.

Going through a typical day you will, as you experience a varied array of thoughts, feelings and emotions give out many different vibrations of energy. As these vibrations go out from you, you attract back to you events, situations and experiences that reflect the same energy. What you give out, you get back. Some teachings and traditions call this karma.

As a golfer and indeed a human being you are giving out many different vibrations of energy depending on what is happening in your life. You may on the morning of a big tournament have an argument with your partner or even your caddy and get very upset, frustrated and angry. As these energies consume you and you feel them deeply you don't realise that you are pulsing out this energy into the universe and it will in someway come back to you.

As the day goes on you may have completely forgot about the aggravating situation earlier on and be totally focussed on your round of golf when suddenly out of the blue something goes wrong. Your drive fizzles off to the right and gets lost in the trees.

'Where did that come from', flashes into your mind, as you feel frustrated and annoyed. Well it's your earlier energy coming back to you. That's how it works, you give it out and you get it back. It doesn't follow any set rules as to how and when it will come back to you but it will come back to you in some negative form.

You may think how can an argument with my caddy result in a wayward drive an hour later? Believe me it can and it does. Think of the energy that you give out as a wave of energy, which is vibrating at a particular frequency and when it has left you it will return in like form, as an experience in your life reflecting the same or similar vibration of energy.

You will probably feel for example disappointed, angry and upset when you get a parking ticket. The next day you encounter more negativity, when you appeal against the ticket but it is upheld and you have to pay the fine. The negative energy generated by getting the parking ticket has returned and created more negativity in your life through the experience of having to pay the fine.

If you hadn't allowed yourself to feel angry, disappointed and upset when you got the parking ticket you would not have pulsed that energy frequency out into the universe and you may well have had your ticket rescinded when you appealed because that energy would not have been out there. Fanciful thinking you may say but this has happened to me on five occasions when I have understood how it works and controlled my emotions at the initial moment when I received the ticket.

Incredible to think that can happen but it does and we are all doing it all of the time without realising. Every time we feel negative about whatever we are pulsing out that vibrational energy into the universe and at some point later it will return to us in like form. Of course because there is usually a time delay we never make the connection so we just keep on doing it, putting our misfortune down to bad luck or whatever. This keeps us lurching from one negative event to another all fuelled by our thoughts and feelings and lots of us experience this everyday of our lives.

Managing your mind all of the time is an important part of your game. If you don't generate negative energy, you can't get it back so why would you want to do it. It is very important that you focus on constantly creating the most positive energy possible if you are to be able to play golf at your best. Little outbursts of anger and frustration on the course simply come back to you in more negative experiences. An angry feeling at having missed a putt could easily result in a miss hit iron shot on the next hole.

At this moment in time everybody is doing it because they don't understand the consequences, so everybody is in the same boat. Even the top professionals don't have a strategy for managing negative energy because they don't realise exactly how it works.

High vibrational thinking shows us how it all works and this empowers you to do something about it. Learn to monitor your thinking and your game will benefit. Keeping a calm mind is beneficial to your game. You should have a strategy to always try your best to give out the correct energy. If you're not putting negativity out there it can't come back to hurt you.

Remember the world is like a mirror and reflects back to you the exact energy that you send out and it comes back in experiences that mirror the same energy frequency.

Get angry over your tax bill, four hours later you miss a vital putt that costs you your purse or the club championship creating more anger. Remain calm and relaxed when you get your tax bill because you know not to let the urge to be angry draw you in, you sink the putt and win the championship, again feeling happy and relaxed.

Being happy, calm and relaxed brings more happy, calm and relaxed events, situations and experiences.

Being angry, frustrated and upset brings more angry, frustrating and upsetting events, situations and experiences.

It's simple really but the key is knowing how it all works. I am sure you all know golfers that have an aggressive or negative temperament and you will see how their tendency to generate negative energy comes back to them.

They are making it hard for themselves and putting obstacles in their own way by their mentality. If they can become more relaxed and calm they will certainly experience more success.

Mind management on the golf course and indeed in the rest of your life is vital if you are to free yourself up to play golf at your very best. Many golfers are their own worst enemy and they don't even realise it.

The Technique

You should always be looking to give out the most positive energy that you can and this should extend into every area of your life. However on the day that you play golf we can draw up a routine to ensure you at least on that day carefully monitor your energy output, which will in turn improve your chances of turning in a good performance.

Starting your day with a meditation would be very helpful to set the correct mindset and the driftwood meditation in module four would be ideal. This will help you to relax and attain a calm serene state of mind, which guarantees you are generating the right type of energy. Once your mood is set with the help of the meditation you need to hold that state of mind for the day and during your round of golf.

Awareness of how energy works is key to you not engaging any potentially negative incidents as you go through the day. Pulsing out feelings of peace and serenity is the best way to ensure that you don't get any nasty surprises during your round of golf.

Managing your mind during the game is also vital to keep the correct energy flowing. You must resist any urges to feel frustrated, angry or whatever during your round no matter what happens.

Self-discipline is vital if you are to master the art of energy output and the more you practice, the better you will get. Make sure on the day of an important round you have nothing that can pop up and surprise you.

Don't bother with opening any unexpected envelopes or take any stressful phone calls, have a relaxing bath, meditate, walk in nature, run, practice breathing exercises. Be careful what type of movies, TV programmes or computer games you subject yourself to. Stay away from newspapers and the news on TV. You don't want anything negative to enter your mind. Peace and tranquillity is the key. It doesn't take a lot of imagination to organise yourself a simple routine that keeps the negativity away and gets you in the right mood for the day.

This is the key, design a tournament day routine that gets you in the high vibrational zone. Stay away from negative people or situations and find what works for you to attain the correct serene, peaceful mindset. Be aware of what energy you are putting out there and modify your thoughts, feelings and emotions to keep the ship steady.

Example of approach to your day:

1. Rise early and have a walk in nature or short jog.

2. Light breakfast followed by a relaxing bath with candles.

3. Driftwood meditation for ten minutes as per module 4.

4. Practice before your round focus on holding serenity and inner peace and using module 7 the inner lake technique.

5. Play a great round of relaxing golf no matter how big the tournament making sure you don't allow negative feelings to infect you no matter what happens during your round.

6. If you are in contention on the final nine holes and sense inner turbulence coming into play drop into your prepared logic plan to steady the energies.

This kind of approach to your day will ensure you are giving yourself the best possible chance of playing golf at your very best even maybe slipping into the high zone. Getting your mind in the right place is vital if you are to achieve your true potential. As with anything practice makes perfect, the more you practice controlling your mind the better you will get.

You have spent years training your golf swing, now you must put the same effort into training your mind. Remember when you first picked up a golf club you weren't as good as you are today, you worked at it and that's what got you to the level you are at today. The same applies to your mind, work at it and you will get better and better.

Ideally in the future when a person starts playing golf and learning how to swing a club they will also start to learn how to think on the golf course. This will bring the physical and mental sides of the game on together and top golfers of the future having trained mind and body will astound you with their ability. Up until now it has been all physical and very little mind training and that applies to the top professionals and amateurs.

High vibrational thinking brings a new understanding to the mind game and will form a solid foundation on which to build the elite professionals of the future. Now that you understand the principles using HVT in your life will become second nature, as you learn to control your impulsive reactions to engage negative energy. This calmer relaxed outlook in time will become your natural state of mind and that's when you will see your ability to play golf consistently at your best really come into fruition.

It's all very simple all you have to remember is what you put out you get back. So keep an eye on the energy that you are generating and always try to keep it as high vibrational as possible. You really don't want any form of negative thinking to enter your mind.

Chapter 15

How it works on the golf course

"Golf is the loneliest sport. You're completely alone with every conceivable opportunity to defeat yourself. Golf brings out your assets and liabilities as a person. The longer you play, the more certain you are that a man's performance is the outward manifestation of who, in his heart, he really thinks he is."

-Hale Irwin-

Hale S. Irwin is an American professional golfer. He was one of the world's leading golfers from the mid-1970s to the mid-1980s

Now you understand the Ten Modules and why you need to get your mind into the correct high vibrational place to achieve peak performance, I will take you through an example of a few holes on the golf course to show you how it may typically work out (this is a fictitious example and not taken from real events).

First I will look at it without using any of the techniques to show you the 'normal' way that a game of golf may go (which I am sure we have all experienced) then I will briefly run through the same scenario again using some of the techniques to show how different it can be when you follow the modules to get yourself in as high a 'zone' as possible.

I will use four good pals of mine to illustrate this example, Neil Chappell, Colin Chappell, Kenny Lahney and Kevan Waggott four keen amateur golfers who I often play a round with.

On this day let's imagine they were playing in a four ball at our local course Seaton Carew, which is a championship links course on the north east coast of England. Seaton is part of a larger town called Hartlepool and the tenth oldest course in England and often regarded as one of the best links courses in the UK and well worth a visit. Their game was usually filled with friendly banter and a keen sense of competitiveness.

On the first tee 'The Rocket' the 360 yard par four a straight drive was essential to stay clear of the out of bounds on the right and the rough undulating ground to the left. It was prudent to take it easy on this hole and just make sure you got your ball in the fairway. You wouldn't say it was a difficult hole but the green was guarded by two deep bunkers one either side and a dip in the fairway directly in front of the bunkers.

Neil hit a fine drive straight down the middle coming to rest in the fairway just before the dip, perfectly placed. Colin did even better and drove his ball down into the dip just in front of the green and Kevan put a bit of a slice on his shot running into the rough on the right but still okay. Kenny hit his signature trade mark 'banana drive' way out to the left fading round into the centre of the fairway, a great controlled shot that only Kenny could pull off.

Kevan was first to play and scrambled his second shot between the bunkers coming to rest twenty feet from the pin, a pretty good result from there. Kenny was next hitting a fine seven iron onto the back of the green. Neil took out his wedge and managed to top the ball straight into the left hand bunker, **'damn'** he cursed banging his club onto the ground. Colin knocked a lovely pitch and run up onto the green running to within six feet of the pin.

After two shots to get out of the bunker you could see Neil was getting **frustrated** and **annoyed**. The others putted out for two pars and a birdie for Colin and Neil finished the first hole with a two over six, **not** a **happy** chap.

The next hole is a long par five called 'Long Trail' again out of bounds to the right and rough to the left. Colin hit a nice drive straight down the middle and Kenny faded one not quite as far but in the fairway. Kevan went for it and hit a beauty thirty yards past everyone, when Kevan connected it flew and Neil feeling a little tense after the first hole opted to take his rescue club for safety and put it not too far but nicely on the fairway.

As they wandered up to play their second shots Kenny's phone rang and he hurriedly pulled it from his bag and pressed the answer button (realising he shouldn't really have left in on). It was work and some sort of problem was going on that involved him and this soon had him **stressed** and **uptight**.

As Kenny lined up his second shot he felt a little out of sorts as his head was still in a spin with what was going on at work and this showed as he shanked his shot over to the right and in the deep rough. After a poor third shot that barely went ten feet Kenny managed in **sheer frustration** to dig it out just onto the edge of the fairway but was still left with almost three hundred yards to go and he had already taken four shots.

Different story for the other guys Kevan hit a brilliant three wood and was just short of the green and Colin did even better and was on the green for two. Neil feeling settled after his conservative tee shot hit the front of the green with two more rescue club shots and was nicely placed for three. Kenny still a little **agitated** managed to get up and onto the front edge of the green for six. All putts down finished with another birdie for Colin a par for Kevan and Neil and a **struggling** eight for Kenny.

The third hole is a testing par three known as 'The Doctor' and the only original hole still in play from when the course was first designed over 140 years ago in 1874. Colin teed up and went to his bag for his eight iron 'oh no I must have left it on the practice range' he blurted out. This **annoyed** Colin as his eight iron was one of his favourite clubs and he didn't like the thought of playing a round without it, let alone the thought of losing it. He went with his nine iron and hit a pretty good looking shot but the wind caught it and it dropped short in one of the very steep bunkers in front of the green. Colin wasn't amused and he felt another surge of **anger** at the thought of leaving behind his eight iron and messing his shot up.

The other guys hit good shots onto the green except Kenny who was still feeling a little **disappointed** after his eight and this showed as he faded it to the right of the green in the light rough, leaving a tricky shot up to an elevated sloping green. He knew even if he hit a good shot it would be almost impossible to stop it rolling on past the hole.

Neil and Kevan putted out for two decent pars and Colin hit a pretty good bunker shot but it scooted on past the hole down the slope on to the far edge of the green much to Colin's **disappointment.** Kenny managed to get it onto the green but again it shot off down the slope just missing the bunker at the side of the green.

Colin pitched up leaving it twelve feet short and two putted for an **irritating** five and Kenny scuffed it onto the green and three putted for a **frustrating** six.

The fourth is 'The Dunes' a short par four of approx 355 yards bending slightly to the right, flanked by sand dunes to the right covered in deep rough and shorter more manageable rough to the left. Anywhere on the right leaves a very testing shot to the green as it is protected by a bunker and almost impossible to hit and stay on the green from there. The correct approach is from the left hand side of the fairway this opens up the green and gives you a clear shot in.

Neil teed off first and put a little too much fade on the drive and curled it over to the right hand rough not the place to be. Kevan next and he gave it an almighty smash fizzing even further over to the right and in a worse position than Neil. They were both **agitated** at the thought of having to try to hit the green from there. Kenny and Colin made the fairway with quite good but conservative drives.

Kevan couldn't find his ball and unfortunately had to go back and play three off the tee, he was **disgruntled** at the thought of this but **trudged** back to tee off again. He tentatively hit a three wood onto the fairway but only to about 175 yards. Neil ended up in the bunker and I don't think Kenny's comment of 'watch out for the bunker Neil' helped just as he was about to play his shot. Colin and Kenny made the front edge of the green in two.

Kevan scraped on for five and was left with a thirty foot putt, he hit a good one that hit the hole but somehow stayed out and ended up three feet away, he popped that in for a **disappointing** seven. Neil did his cigar advert impersonation and took three in the bunker eventually squirting out and two putting for an **annoying** seven. Colin two putted for a par and Kenny three putted for a five.

Now I could go on and tell you about what happened on every hole but it was more or less the same story, some great shots, plenty of not so great shots, some harsh words and plenty of off putting banter and mickey taking. Overall it was a typical round for these guys more or less playing to their handicap or just over. Nine times out of ten this is how they played but occasionally one of them would have a great round and better their handicap, somehow on that day playing at an altogether higher level.

I expect this is how most people find their golf goes most of the time average, sometimes terrible but every now and then the magic happens and they play that amazing special round of golf.

Generally they are playing golf under the powerful influence of their inner resistance, if I could reach into their minds and take out their inner resistance just for one round of golf you would see miracles happening.

Unfortunately this is what we are all doing whether we are playing golf or simply living our everyday lives; we are constantly under the heavy negative influence of our inner resistance.

The secret is getting rid of your inner resistance and this will raise your vibration and improve your golf beyond what you can possibly imagine and this applies to amateurs and professionals.

Chapter 16

How it works using the modules

"No matter how good you get, you can always get better — and that's the exciting part."

-Tiger Woods-

Eldrick Tont "Tiger" Woods is an American professional golfer who is among the most successful golfers of all time

Now let's have a look at the same day but with a difference, this time let's assume the guys read this book first and were following some of the modules. I will just concentrate on the shots that are different due to the better mental approach to the game.

On the first tee Neil hit a fine drive straight down the middle coming to rest in the fairway just before the dip, perfectly placed. For his next shot he took out his wedge and managed to top the ball straight into the left hand bunker, **'damn'** he cursed banging his club onto the ground.

Neil realised he was allowing negative energy to infect his mind so he took three deeps breaths to calm himself then applied his favourite module for getting himself into the 'high zone' module 4. Saying the trigger word 'driftwood' in his mind helps him slip into a serene, peaceful mindset and this raises his vibration up to, or nearer to the 'high zone' and this helps him to let the negative feelings float away.

Then he hit a good bunker shot landing the ball only around seven feet from the pin and he finished the first hole with a tricky seven footer but he had a lot of faith in his old two ball Alien putter and hit it perfect and got his par, great result.

The next hole the long par five Kenny hit an okay drive onto the fairway. As they wandered up to play their second shots Kenny's phone rang and he hurriedly pulled it from his bag and pressed the answer button (realising he shouldn't really have left in on). It was work and some sort of problem was going on that involved him and this soon had him **stressed** and **uptight**.

As Kenny lined up his second shot he felt a little out of sorts as his head was still in a spin with what was going on at work and this showed as he shanked his shot over to the right and into the deep rough. After a poor third shot that barely went ten feet Kenny managed in **sheer frustration** to dig it out just onto the edge of the fairway but was still left with almost three hundred yards to go and he had already taken four shots.

Kenny still a little **agitated** managed to get up and onto the front edge of the green for six.

At this point Kenny sensed he had become negative and took three deep breaths to settle himself then he used module 8. and opted to alter his perspective and expectations for the putt. He visualised and felt the feelings of his putt going in instead of going with the normal expectation of hopefully two or even three putting.

He hit a beauty and sank the putt rattling it around the cup before it dropped in for a shot saving seven.

On the third hole Colin teed up and went to his bag for his eight iron 'oh no I must have left it on the practice range' he blurted out. This **annoyed** Colin as his eight iron was one of his favourite clubs and he didn't like the thought of playing a round without it, let alone the thought of losing it. He went with his nine iron and hit a pretty good looking shot but the wind caught it and it dropped short in one of the very steep bunkers in front of the green. Colin wasn't amused and he felt another surge of **anger** at the thought of leaving behind his eight iron and messing his shot up.

The other guys hit good shots onto the green except Kenny who was still feeling a little **disappointed** after his seven (still carrying some negative energy) and this showed as he faded it to the right of the green in the light rough, leaving a tricky shot up to an elevated sloping green. He knew even if he hit a good shot it would be almost impossible to stop it rolling on past the hole. Colin hit a pretty good bunker shot but it scooted on past the hole down the slope on to the far edge of the green much to Colin's **disappointment.** Kenny managed to get it onto the green but again it shot off down the slope just missing the bunker at the side of the green.

Colin noted the sense of disappointment and took three deep breaths to calm himself and then thought about module 9. 'The logic plan' with this in mind he concentrated on his plan for two putts and getting the first putt into the ten foot circle then finishing with a visualisation of the sunken cup.

This focussed his mind and helped him relax letting go of the negative feelings and pushing up his vibration in the process.

This paid off and Colin rolled it within two feet and sank the putt for a not too bad bogey four.

At this point Kenny also realised he had become negative again so he took three deep breaths to settle himself and then he used module 6. to alter his 'perspective' and expectations for the shot and letting go of the negative energy in the process. He visualised and felt the feelings of his shot going in and hit a lovely chip and roll coming to rest eight inches from the hole, he popped that in for an excellent four.

On the fourth Kevan gave it an almighty smash fizzing over to the right and in a worse position than Neil. They were both **agitated** at the thought of having to try to hit the green from there. Kevan couldn't find his ball and unfortunately had to go back and play three off the tee, he was **disgruntled** at the thought of this but **trudged** back to tee off again.

At this point he realised he was feeling quite negative and that this would drag down his vibration away from the 'high zone' making it even more difficult. So he took three deep breaths and calmed himself before thinking of module 10. 'Energy in / energy out' this allowed him to let go of the negative feelings and calm himself generating more positive energy which in turn helped his vibration to rise. And he knew getting his vibration up was key to staying as close to the 'high zone' as possible and letting go of this negative blip.

Feeling decidedly calmer Kevan took out his three wood and hit a nice smooth drive 225 yards down the centre of the fairway and it finished up perfect just rolling over to the left hand side. Neil ended up in the bunker and I don't think Kenny's comment of 'watch out for the bunker Neil' helped just as he was about to play his shot, Kenny was an expert at making a comment at the right time just to put that thought into your head but this was all part and parcel of the fun.

Kevan hit a good iron onto the green ten feet from the pin and holed the putt for a very respectable five.

Neil calmed himself thinking again **'driftwood'** before hitting a brilliant bunker shot that rattled the pin coming to rest a couple of feet away enabling him to pop it in for a satisfying par.

Analysis

As you can see the examples I have given you show just what a difference training yourself to be in a high vibrational mindset could have. You will have more luck, hole more putts and lower your scores using these techniques. All of the lads played better when using the modules and lowered their scores and this is exactly how it works. Normally we have no knowledge of what's going on and no strategy to counteract the negative energies that inevitably pop up and therefore we are damaged by whatever negativity is around. The majority of us are playing our golf with very little thought to our mindset and unknowingly paying the price.

Can you imagine what damage you can sustain when, for example you have an argument with your partner before a round or are going through some other external difficulties in your life? You can end up taking to the golf course in a state of anxiety, stress or tension which drags you down the vibrations putting you in the worst possible mindset to play golf and I bet we have all experienced this.

Negative energy free is the key to attaining and staying in the 'high zone' or as close to it as possible.

We have all seen the top professionals on TV winning major championships and some of them excelling at this, Bubba Watson, Tiger Woods, Rory McIlroy, Sergio Garcia, and Phil Mickelson etc. You may say they are the best of the best because they handle the pressure when it matters but that means they are better at not letting negative energy affect them. In other words they are better at keeping themselves in a high a vibrational state than the rest. This enables them to hold their form when it matters most.

Now you know how it all works and whether you are a club golfer playing in the monthly medal or a professional in contention on the back nine in a major, you can use these techniques to hold yourself in or as close to the 'high zone' as possible, maximising your chance of playing at your very best.

Understanding how it all works and then using the modules that suit you is how you begin doing this. I believe Module 1. Following the Notebook is essential for everybody who is serious about learning how to attain the 'high zone'. This is the basic

'The mind game finally explained'

exercise that will get working on releasing that inner resistance and get you up the vibrations.

Next I would recommend Module 2, to enlist the help of your inner child, another powerful tool to overcome your most stubborn and hard to break down inner resistance. Then it's up to you to choose which other modules best suit you to use before or during your game. They will all help you but you may find you favour one technique over the others so put your effort into practicing that one.

My favourite is Module 7 'the inner lake', I find this easy to build into my routine and it helps me to settle down the energies whenever I am about to play a shot. This is the module that helped me return my best ever nine holes score on my home course Seaton Carew, a par 36 for the difficult back nine in testing conditions. And I had not practiced the technique prior to this day, I had written about it but this was the first time I had tried to actually use it on the golf course, so it can't be that difficult to use once you understand how it works.

I had a terrible 54 on the front nine and then realised I wasn't using my own techniques I was just playing golf like everybody else and at the mercy of whatever energies were buffeting me, so I quickly started using Module 7 and played an unbelievable back nine.

Everything just clicked into place as I used the module to find my inner peace and serenity before each shot and this day it worked a treat, three birdies, three pars and three bogeys. My handicap is 18 so this for me was a revelation especially after a disastrous front nine in cold, windy conditions and a total example of how well the modules do and can work and believe me the back nine at Seaton is a test for anybody, its far more difficult than the front nine.

Mind management is the key and if you have been playing your golf without a strategy to get your mind into the best possible place, you will see huge improvements once you start employing some of these techniques.

Golf is not just about getting the ball into the hole but also about searching for and holding the correct mindset while you are doing it. When you practice and bring these two things together your game will improve beyond your highest expectations.

"Tempo is the glue that s...

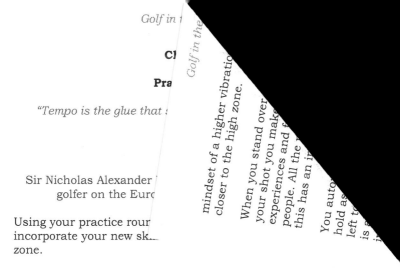

Sir Nicholas Alexander ...
golfer on the Euro...

Using your practice rour...
incorporate your new sk...
zone.

For this example I have adapted module 7 'The inner lake' technique although of course you can use any of the modules that you prefer. It's excellent to set the right mindset and learn how to hold it which is vital if you are to master getting into and staying in the high zone. The same technique is applied to all the shots.

Remember the more you practice this technique the better you will get at slipping into the mindset of the high zone, you have to train your mind to attain the high zone and hold it during your round just as you have to practice your golf swing and striking a golf ball. I will start with driving then work through the other various shots.

Driving

The higher your vibration, in other words the closer you are to the high zone the easier it is for you to consistently hit longer, straighter drives.

What makes you lose yardage and accuracy is the negative influence of your inner resistance.

This is where the shimmers of negative energy are generated from that result in lost yardage and wayward shots; you must learn to control and overcome your inner resistance to consistently hit longer more accurate drives. And the way to do that is to rise above it to a higher vibration therefore leaving its influence behind. It can't negatively affect you when you are in a n and this is when you are in or

a drive and look down the fairway picturing
instant judgments based on your previous
rom what you have learned by observing other
revious data you have stored comes into play and
fluence on the shot you are about to play.

matically assess all the relevant information that you
you look at the shot, which is the best type of drive to hit,
right, right to left, straight, long or short etc. The problem
ll the information you are automatically assessing in an
nstant is also infused with all the negative information you have
stored about your driving abilities and the potential pitfalls.

And the further down in vibration that you are at that moment the more negative energy you will have to contend with. This looks a long way? That bunker is in the way? Don't want to go in the trees? Out of bounds to the right? I'm not confident with my driver? I hope I don't slice it? I'm two shots clear; I hope I don't make a mistake? And so on.

These negative thoughts, which bubble up quite naturally and often so subtly that you hardly even notice them create negative feelings and these feelings are what contain the tension, anxiety and mild apprehension etc that drag you down the vibrations and mess with your potential to execute the perfect shot.

In fact you might not even be able to detect any thoughts as such, it's simply experienced as a sudden slight change in your mindset or a slight dip in your general overall feeling and anything could trigger it. Your last shot, a memory of playing this hole before, a previous poor shot you have hit, the wind changing etc, and it usually happens so subtly that you can barely detect it.

This is what happens to many of the world's top professional golfers on the home stretch of a major. The shimmers of negative energy enter the equation 'can I really win a major', 'am I really leading a Major' etc and this pulls them down fractionally in vibration, which loses them their form slightly. The next thing you know it's got a grip of them the negative energy is flooding in and it's all going wrong.

And there is no other club in your bag as prolific as your driver to get it all started. It's astonishing the amount of information you process just standing over your drive and more than any other club it will spark off your inner resistance flooding you with negative thoughts and feelings. It is the most stressful club in the bag to use in terms of triggering off the inner turbulence.

When all this information rushes into your mind you can very easily be lost in the static and hit a poor shot. You must train yourself to ignore the attempts of your inner resistance to create inner turmoil and focus on positive thoughts and feelings especially when using your driver.

Hours and hours of practice minimise the effects of inner resistance because you come to know what you can do. You become certain of your ability to play the shot. You believe.

It stands to reason that if you are faced with a difficult drive and you have hardly played golf that you will not have the same confidence that a professional golfer, who has hit thousands of similar drives will have.

You would be wide open for your inner resistance to generate doubts about you hitting a good shot. The professional golfer would be more or less certain that he would hit a good shot. So out of twenty attempts the result could well be something like, you hit six fairways and the pro hits sixteen.

His beliefs are better than yours because he has put the practice time in and probably is more talented so this has eliminated his doubts. He believes more. His inner resistance in this instance (concerning hitting a drive) is less powerful and carries less negative energy and floods his mind less.

So when faced with a drive less shimmers of negativity arise in his mind and body enhancing his chances of hitting a good shot. If you had no inner resistance you would massively increase your chances of hitting every drive long and into the perfect place on the fairway.

I read a book many years ago called 'Zen and the Art of Archery'. In this book a German Professor was working in Japan and he joined an archery club. It was six years before they even let him hold the bow. It was all about firing the arrow without any inner resistance getting in the way in other words about attaining the high zone. This way you could more consistently attain peak performance.

One day the archery teacher showed him how it was done and fired an arrow blindfolded into the dead centre of the target. Then he repeated the feat with the lights turned off splitting the first arrow. Impossible you may think but in fact it is absolutely possible.

The teacher said the secret is, you don't shoot the arrow, it shoots itself. This means you don't consciously shoot the arrow because you are consciously focused on holding your inner peace and serenity, this is where your attention is, this allows your subconscious to take control and shoot the arrow.

You experience it as stepping aside consciously, which gives you a sort of detached feeling, as you contemplate inner peace and serenity. Then you 'feel' the shot naturally happen as your subconscious mind fires the shot.

When playing golf this should be your focus and you hardly give the actual shot any real thought or attention. You are aware of the taking the shot but you are so immersed in holding your inner peace and serenity that playing the shot is not even important; you are not attached to the shot. It is secondary to you holding the high zone.

This is where none attachment to the outcome is important to allow your subconscious full control. You don't care whether the drive is good or not, all you care about is holding the feeling of inner peace. Of course you want to hit a good drive but **it's not going to bother you if you don't**, you will simply accept it and move on with no disturbance to your inner peace. If you do hit a poor shot and feel a surge of negativity arising within such as anger, frustration etc, take three deep breaths and let it go.

Mastering this level of mind control is essential to being able to stay in the higher vibrations. You must really and truly not allow any negative emotions to disturb your serene feelings even if the shot does not quite go according to plan. The natural reaction is always disappointment, frustration, annoyance etc and a drop in vibration and you must teach yourself not to let this happen and doing this in your practice rounds is a great way to train your mind to hold the high zone or stay as close to it as possible. Non reaction is the key and a vital part of this discipline and this is how you use your golf not only to practice your game but also to train your mind.

Practicing this technique by-passes your inner resistance and holds you in the correct mindset of the high zone. Hitting a golf ball down a fairway is child's play for your subconscious mind when your inner resistance is out of the way.

Your subconscious mind is immensely powerful in comparison to your conscious mind. The problem is we are living everyday of our lives generally through our conscious mind, which is heavily influenced by our inner resistance and when we play golf we do it mainly using our conscious mind. We are thinking about it all too much, too much analysing, measuring and assessing.

This guarantees our inner resistance will have a negative impact on our game. Learning to hit a drive with your subconscious mind in control and at the same time taking your inner resistance out of the equation allows you to rise in vibration and perform at peak level. This is what is called being in the 'high zone'.

We used to refer to golfers like Seve Ballesteros as somebody who played on 'feel and instinct' because they didn't analyse too much and could play amazing shots. What Seve was really doing was using his subconscious more than most, hence the incredible golf he could play. He was naturally getting in the high zone or close to it and I believe this was due to his love for and childlike excitable approach to the game. Yes he also got angry and frustrated which will have dragged his vibration down but then the next minute he was back up because he had such an eager enthusiasm and passion for every shot. He loved to create wonderful amazing shots and this meant he would whizz back up the vibrations and leave behind the negativity in an instant as he excitedly pondered what magic he could produce next.

You will have experienced the high zone maybe for the odd shot or even for a full round. I remember hitting a perfect drive one day when faced with a really difficult fairway to hit. As I stood over the ball I felt very calm and relaxed and for some strange reason I knew that I would hit a great shot. I even remember thinking I can hit this down the right or the left and it will still work out well.

I had a feeling of certainty about the drive and sure enough I hit a perfect drive. I had somehow let go of my inner resistance and moved my conscious mind to one side and played the shot through my subconscious mind. Just like the archery teacher I was in the correct mindset and achieved an amazing shot way beyond my normal level.

I was in the 'high zone'. I had let go of any negative energy and risen into the 'high zone' and played the shot negative energy free. The usual 'static' was not there. My inner resistance for once was silent. The shot felt easy and relaxed, no real effort, as if I was not putting full power into it.

For you to learn to drive using your subconscious mind like this you must follow a practice that is working on getting rid of your inner resistance, as we have discussed in the first three modules and teach yourself to rise above your conscious mind when hitting your shots using the other modules.

The following is a great technique to use in your practice rounds to train yourself to step aside from your conscious mind when hitting a drive, it's module 7 'The inner lake technique':

When assessing your shot don't think too much about it. Forget all the usual analysing and measuring. No need to worry about all of that because your subconscious knows exactly how to play the shot. When you get into the technicalities of the shot too much you are looking at it through your conscious mind and this opens the door for negative energy to come flooding in. Thinking about it too much can lose you the sense of inner peace that accompanies the high zone.

Instead casually glance down the fairway and allow your subconscious mind to download the data. I sometimes imagine I am taking a snap video of the shot. Don't worry if you think you haven't analysed it enough, your subconscious mind just needs a brief look to download the data.

Then choose a point on the fairway at around the 120-150 yard mark (maybe 200-230 yds for professionals) on what you think may be approx the correct line, pick out a spot and focus on hitting your drive to here. This is your landing point and use the amount of power that you feel will achieve that. This will slow your tempo down and help you to swing inner resistance free. At this point take a couple of deep breaths to settle yourself.

Then as you settle over the ball you must concentrate on feeling calm, serene and peaceful, this must be your focus. Picture the inner lake inside your chest and it's perfectly still, not even the slightest ripple on the surface. Hold that stillness and feel the calm energy of the lake as you prepare for your shot. Then you notice a tiny ripple on the water, concentrate on settling it down until it's perfectly still and you can feel that total stillness inside you.

Any movement on the surface of the water is an indication of negative energy present, try to settle it so its perfectly still this is the skill you must master, don't worry you will soon be able to do this in seconds as part of your usual set-up and it will take no extra time.

At this point you may feel your grip loosen, as if you are barely holding the club it's more or less just resting in your hands.

This is when you are ready to hit your drive.

Still focusing on serenity, inner peace and the perfectly still lake hit your shot with a casual thought of your landing spot 120 yards away and remember you only need the power to get you there that is your target. After the drive has been hit keep focused on holding the feeling of inner peace, keep the lake perfectly still and don't look up to see where the ball has gone. Keep your head down as long as you can till the momentum of your swing pulls you up.

Allowing yourself to look up too early may encourage 'eager anticipation', which may fractionally lose your inner peace and allow negative energy in just as you are executing the shot. This all takes place in milli-seconds so you are not even aware of it happening, the only way to control it is to discipline yourself to keep your head down and still as long as possible.

You will be amazed at how much control and accuracy you have and even more amazed when you see your ball fly way over your landing point and far off into the distance. Smooth tempo is much better than aggressive power, which often ends up going less distance and often into trouble. Amateur golfers certainly should really never unleash full power with the driver especially at the start of a round because this is what will get you into trouble.

Setting a good tempo with your first drive is a great way to start off your round in the best serene mindset. This helps set the correct flow for your round physically and mentally. Even the top professionals often only hit eight or nine out of fourteen fairways with the powerful drivers available today. Getting the tempo right is vital to keep you as close to the high zone as possible.

Practice this technique and you will soon master the art of long accurate driving with your subconscious mind and you will hit drives that you can now only dream about but you must train yourself to rise into the 'High Zone', just the same as you have to train yourself to hit different shots.

To recap here is a brief breakdown of the 'Inner Lake' technique:

1. Casually look at your shot and take a couple of deep breaths.
2. Set up and concentrate on keeping the inner lake still.
3. **Feel** the serenity and inner peace.
4. When you **feel** relaxed and detached from the outcome play the shot.
5. Keep your head down and **'feel'** the ball heading perfectly on target.
6. If you don't hit a great shot **keep the negative emotions out**.

Practice makes perfect.

Immaculate Iron Shots

The same applies equally for your iron shots, the higher your vibration the better your iron shots will be because you will have less negative energy around getting in the way.

Use the same visualisation to settle down any shimmers of negative energy. A brief look at the shot and pay no mind to any negative thoughts that flicker up, just let them float away as you settle into serenity and inner peace. See that lake in your mind and keep the water perfectly still.

Again keep your head down after you have hit the shot to eliminate 'eager anticipation' and try not to look up until you sense that the ball is landing on the green (professionals will be comfortable looking up earlier without problems as they have put the practice in).

As you hold your head still, feel and picture the ball flying perfectly towards the target and do this in a calm relaxed way. No real intense effort, just calm and relaxed, remember at this point as far as your mind is concerned it doesn't matter if you hit a great shot or a bad shot, what matters is holding your serenity and inner peace. Your focus is serenity and inner peace with a casual thought of the ball going on target.

If you practice this with every iron shot that you hit you will soon master the art of getting your mind in the high zone for peak performance. And this is when you will consistently hit iron shots that will astound you.

Perfect chip shots

Same again, the higher your vibration the better your chipping will be.

Don't allow your plan for the shot to be infused with all the potential negatives. This looks a fast green? That bunker is in the way? Don't want to go off the back of the green? Hope I don't fluff the shot? I hope I don't shank it? Etc.

Remember these sort of negative thoughts are where the tension, anxiety and mild apprehension is. Engage in them when they flutter through your mind and your inner resistance has you, you have bought into it and are generating negative thoughts and feelings and that's what it's after.

And when your inner resistance has drawn you in your vibration has dropped and your chances of hitting a good shot are compromised. Again keep your head down after you have hit the shot to eliminate 'eager anticipation' and try not to look up until you feel that the ball is four feet from the hole.

As you hold your head still feel the ball flying perfectly towards the chosen landing spot and running dead on target for the hole. Again stay calm and relaxed, don't engage any negativity that is trying to get your attention, keep the lake perfectly still.

Serenity and inner peace is your focus with an almost casual non caring thought towards the actual shot, remember it doesn't matter if you hit a great chip or a bad chip, what matters is holding your serenity and inner peace.

This is how you play golf in the high zone, golf at your absolute best, you take all the intensity out of it, and you play like it doesn't matter.

Sink any Putt

This is my favourite shot to use this technique on. I have hit some incredible putts using this technique, putts that have astounded me and way beyond my actual talent level.

Putting is all about belief, if you believe it will go in, it will because total belief means no doubt, no negative energy about whether you can sink the putt.

Again casually glance at the putt as you walk up to it allowing your subconscious to download the data. Don't worry if you think you haven't analysed it enough your subconscious just needs a brief look at the shot.

Then as you settle over the putt you must concentrate on feeling calm, serene and peaceful, this must be your focus. See that inner lake inside your chest and keep the water perfectly still.

When you are totally relaxed, serene and the inner lake has settled down you are ready to hit the putt and again this is when you may feel your grip completely relax, this is a good sign that you are ready.

After the putt has been hit keep focused on holding the feeling of inner peace and keep the lake perfectly still and don't look up to see where the ball has gone. Keep your head down and picture the ball travelling to the hole, feel it following a perfect line and see it heading into the centre of the cup. Know with a certainty that the ball will drop into the hole, you know it is in.

When you feel the ball is approximately four feet from the hole you can look up. Again it is very important to follow this discipline while training yourself to use your subconscious mind, you must not look up.

As you know allowing yourself to look up can encourage 'eager anticipation', which can lose your inner peace and allow negative energy in just as you play the shot. The only way to control it is to discipline yourself to keep your head down and still until the ball is four-feet from the hole. This applies equally to a ten-foot putt or a forty-foot putt. I cannot emphasise the importance of this to ensure that you stay in subconscious mode throughout the entire shot.

Practice this and you will soon master the art of putting with your subconscious mind and you will be making putts that you can now only dream about.

So now you have a simple technique that you can use for all of your golf shots. This is all you need to train your mind to get into the 'High Zone' for each shot. Keep practicing it with every shot and before long you will have trained yourself to naturally slip into the high zone and hold it. Then you will see huge improvements in your golf as you more consistently play closer to or at your very best.

Chapter 18

Quantum Golf

"The more I practice, the luckier I get."

-Gary Player-

Gary Player DMS, OIG is a retired South African professional golfer. Over his career, Player accumulated nine major championships on the regular tour and six Champions Tour major championship victories

I have saved the biggest secret till last.

First I want to take you back to Johnny Millers words when he said:

'Tiger's father taught him that if he really believed, he could make things happen'.

So what does this mean 'he could make things happen'?

To explain this we will take a peak into the world of quantum physics and the first thing I need you to understand is the double slit experiment.

The Double Slit Experiment was first conducted by Thomas Young back in 1803 to demonstrate the wave theory of light and the initial aim of the experiment was to fire a single electron at a plate with two slits to see which slit the electron would go through. It was expected that because the electron was a particle it would go through one of the slits and hit the backboard behind. This didn't happen; instead it went through both slits at the same time leaving a pattern of interference on the backboard.

This meant the electron was not acting as a particle but as a wave, however a strange thing happened when an observer was present it began acting like a particle and only went through one of the slits. This meant the observer was affecting the experiment

and turning the wave into a particle simply by the act of observation.

How could this be possible?

It could only be possible if the observer was influencing the electron in some way, which means the observer was somehow influencing reality.

The conclusion is reality is a wave of probability until an observer is present, then dependant on what the observer expects to happen, happens.

Or put another way whatever the observer believes the most is what generally manifests. The observer's beliefs are made up of all that they have experienced up till that point in their lives and this information is held in their conscious and subconscious minds. As they experience things in their lives they project their beliefs onto each given situation and this affects the outcome.

They are not aware most of the time of their core beliefs as they are held deep in their subconscious mind, so they do not realise that they are having a powerful influence on everything that is happening.

What we can deduce from this is we are influencing everything in our lives in this way and that means we are integral in creating what happens in our reality and we are doing this through what we believe.

Well that's mind blowing enough but what has that got to do with golf?

Back to Johnny Millers words about Tigers father telling him if he really believed it he could make things happen.

When you hit a forty foot putt (or indeed any putt or shot) and I advise keeping your head down for as long as possible there is a reason for this other than you may let negative energy seep in at the last minute and it is once you look up you then become the observer and this is when you can still have an influence through your deep seated beliefs.

You can see your ball rolling towards the hole and you may have doubts about whether it will go in and this line of thought creates the corresponding feelings and the feelings are the energy source that can still impact the putt negatively and **make it miss**.

Everything is energy remember and as in all forms of energy one form can affect another, in quantum physics this is called quantum entanglement (see foot note).

Sounds crazy but this is how it works, you can still affect the outcome after you have hit the ball. Now I am not saying this is what happens every time you look at your ball in motion but the fact is that you can when the circumstances come together have an influence in making things happen positively or negatively. And please remember it is not just me saying this, it is all backed up by quantum physics.

On the positive side this means you can also have an influence on the ball when it is going to possibly miss and instead make it teeter on the edge then drop into the hole, hence Tiger's father's advice. He knew something and made Tiger aware of it.

In fact I believe he taught Tiger this from an early age which left him with high expectations or beliefs that things would work out for him, so therefore he ended up carrying less inner resistance than most in respect of sinking long putts, chips etc explaining his uncanny ability to land more than his fair share of these shots.

He believed he could do it and he never wavered in this belief, so when the ball looked like it wasn't going in and the majority of us would have accepted that therefore generating the corresponding feelings, he still had the belief and equally as importantly the feelings that it might and for him it sometimes did.

For the rest of us it's a different story because when we look at the ball rolling towards the hole we normally do it with the interference of our inner resistance and this negative part of us is only too keen to promote what may go wrong and not what will go right and this can have an adverse affect on what we feel resulting in things maybe not working out for us.

Although if you are in the high zone and feeling calm and at peace you will have less inner resistance getting in the way when you look and in this instance you may find your own touch of magic helping the ball into the hole.

So when you are taking your shot unless you are in the high zone it is prudent not to look up too early and then you will not be potentially interfering in a negative way with the outcome. Keep your head down as long as possible and try to really believe and feel that it is going in the hole; this is the best approach to apply and this focus will help keep your inner resistance quiet.

If you feel that you are in a high enough mindset ie: the high zone or close to it then looking early should not have an adverse effect and you just might add momentum to the shot and make it happen.

Belief is the key, if you 100% believe it will go in it will, this is what you must work on; making yourself believe, this is a mindset that has no doubts.

Albert Einstein said it perfectly:

'Everything is energy and that is all there is to it. Match the frequency of the reality that you want and you can not help but get that reality. It can be no other way. This is not philosophy. This is physics'.

So match the frequency of the ball dropping in the hole and that is what you will get. This means you must feel the ball has already dropped into the hole and you are having the joyful feelings associated with that and you must do this as the ball rolls towards the hole. Just jump forward a few frames and see the ball dropping in the cup. Celebrate in your mind as if it has already happened. Believe it and very importantly **feel it**. And this mini visualisation is not done with effort, intensity and excessive determined focus; it is best done from the mindset of the high zone.

It's almost casually done with no real effort involved you just hold your peace and serenity and picture it dropping in the cup and let the gentle happy **feelings** wash over you. And remember if it misses you have no negative feeling reaction, simply accept it and then you hold onto the high zone. It's about rising above the tense negative energy of your inner resistance and holding yourself in a state of peace as you softly picture the desired result. This positive visualisation of the end result with the associated gentle happy **feelings** will help create exactly that and suddenly you will be the guy that sinks the amazing shots.

Remember belief is the key and it's the **feelings** (the energy) generated from that belief that creates the magic; this is what you must practice.

And this is why you need to always be in the best possible high vibrational mindset when you are playing so you are already up there close to the high vibrational doubt free energy of belief. To go from a negative state such as frustration or disappointment to absolute belief is a big jump up the vibrations and more difficult to achieve. The higher you are vibrating initially the better your little visualisation will work. It's about tweaking your vibration through positive visualisation to attain the **feelings** of certain belief and this is the energy that will power things into being, this is the secret.

This is how you make things happen.

Entanglement takes place when a part of particles interact physically. In quantum physics, entangled particles remain connected so that actions performed by one affects the behaviour of the other, even if they are separated by huge distances. The phenomenon so riled Albert Einstein he called it "spooky action at a distance."

https://www.google.co.uk/search?q=quantum+entanglement&rlz=1C1AOHY_en-GBGB709GB709&oq

Chapter 19

Golf Psychology

"A bad attitude is worse than a bad swing."

-Payne Stewart-

William Payne Stewart was an American professional golfer who won eleven PGA Tour events, including three major championships in his career

The new perspective that high vibrational thinking brings to golf psychology will allow new methods to be developed, which can help players from every level. The following is a look at various scenarios from a HVT point of view to demonstrate its versatility and unique approach.

One of my favourite golf psychology books is 'Golf is not a game of perfect' by Dr Bob Rotella; it's a brilliant book and well worth a read. In the book he gives an example of a golfer playing in the 'high zone'. Chip Beck carded a 59 in an official tournament and when asked about his state of mind that day his reply was *'he had a serene feeling of confidence as the round progressed'* and *'I stayed out of my way for the whole day'*.

Dr Rotella clarified his comment about staying out of his own way as *'not allowing any doubts into his mind'*.

Looking at this from a HVT perspective Chip Beck had detached himself slightly from what was going on whilst holding the mindset of serenity and inner peace, which allowed him to play the round in the 'high zone'. Holding the correct mindset enabled the serene feeling of confidence to continue and this kept low vibrational negative energy out of his mind.

He played the round without buying into the usual range of negative thoughts that might pop up and this kept him in the higher vibrations. He kept his conscious mind out of the way and let it happen and this kept him up the vibrations and in the 'high zone'. Look at the result an astonishing 59.

"For this game you need, above all things, to be in a tranquil frame of mind."

-Harry Vardon-

'The mind game finally explained'

One of the all time great professional golfer's from the Bailiwick of Jersey

In another chapter Dr Rotella talks about 'choking' he describes it as:

'A golfer chokes when he lets anger, doubt, fear or some other extraneous factor distract him before a shot'.

This can result in a multitude of physical reactions, tensing up, stiffness, loss of grace etc and ultimately a poor shot.

Again from a HVT viewpoint negative energy has been allowed in by the golfer engaging the negative thoughts popping up in his mind (which bubble up from his inner resistance) and buying into them emotionally has then created the associated negative **'feelings'**, anger, doubt, fear etc and this facilitates a drop in vibration making it difficult for him to play the shot that he normally would execute without any problem.

The allowing in of negativity drags the player down into a lower vibrational place where it becomes difficult for him to play the shot; this is often called 'choking' when it happens over a very important shot (a classic inner resistance move to step up the pressure when it really matters). The answer of course is get your conscious mind occupied with something that creates good feelings or focuses on good feelings and let the negative thoughts that are bubbling up just drift away without becoming emotionally entangled in them. Be ready for them and ignore them.

When you are in the higher vibrations everything flows perfectly, your swing is easy, fluent and you are supple and relaxed. A good analogy would be it's like playing on a beautiful summers day in your polo shirt. Whereas in the lower vibrations its like trying to swing the club with four shirts on, three jumpers and two jackets, you feel constricted, awkward and out of sorts. The further down in vibration you get the more difficult it is or metaphorically speaking the more jackets you have on.

Dr Rotella also talks about Severiano Ballesteros; Seve had tinkered with his swing in order to chase his dream of winning the US Open. This tinkering had opened the door for too much thinking and analysing and this had allowed negativity to seep in. Dr Rotella explained to Seve that he needed to go back to being Seve and play how he used to play, from the heart, he had to re-capture being the 'artist' as this was his natural way.

HVT shows us that Seve had allowed negativity in by focussing on the mechanics of his swing; the technicalities and this had dragged down his vibration. There is always a danger of this when you consciously assess something in great detail, too much 'what if', 'should I do this,' 'what if I try that' etc, especially when you are such a 'feel' player as he was. This sort of conscious mind analytical thinking leaves the door wide open for negative energy in the form of worry, stress, confusion, anger, frustration etc and it's very difficult to stop it once it starts to seep in.

This presented his inner resistance with an opportunity to spark into life because he was now operating much more through his conscious mind instead of how he naturally played, which was mainly in the higher vibrations and often through the subconscious. He had changed from playing with a high vibrational mindset of wonder, joy, excitement and enthusiasm to a lower vibrational mindset of intense critical thinking.

And for Seve this was disastrous, his new approach to golf was dragging him down in vibration and ultimately messing with his form; you cannot play in the lower vibrations as well as you can play in the higher vibrations, especially a player like Seve who is naturally a player that relies on instinct and feel and playing from the higher zones rather than a conscious analytical percentage golf type of approach.

The answer I would have given Seve is:

'Get your conscious mind out of the way by focussing it on holding serenity and inner peace, this will keep it occupied and create the right feelings and at the same time this will help raise your vibration.

Then while you are predominantly and consciously holding yourself in this good feeling place, casually assess each shot without thinking too much about it, in other words go back to your natural way of playing relying more on feel and instinct.

This relaxed approach will allow the natural you to re-emerge flooding you with the energies that make you who you truly are, energies such as passion, excitement, creativity, childlike enthusiasm and your genuine love for the game, which you had lost or drowned out due to concentrating too much on the technical elements. And these energies are your secret to the higher vibrations and the reason why when coupled up with your god given natural talent you have the magic and can hit the wonderful shots that you do.

To put it bluntly stop being so serious and let your excitement for the game back in, enjoy yourself this is how you get your form back'.

Exactly what Dr Rotella advised him to do in different words of course.

Essentially Seve was naturally playing much of his golf in the higher vibrations and he achieved this because of his excitable passion and sheer wonder for the game he loved so much. Simply put he embodied high vibrational thoughts and feelings on the golf course because he enjoyed playing so much and he was eager to see what magic he could conjure up next and this enthusiastic mentality lifted him up the vibrations. To Seve golf was not just a game, it was an expression of who he was, he truly was an artist on the golf course. Golf was his joy.

And given his emotional approach to the game in the sense of him also expressing his disappointments and frustrations every round must have been for him an incredible roller coaster ride up and down the energy spectrum. Severiano Ballesteros in full flow was a spectacle to behold, anything could happen and it usually did. I believe he was the most naturally gifted and exciting creative golfer we have ever seen.

Module 7 'The inner lake' would have been ideal for Seve to follow to give him the best focus to allow his natural game to come back and leave behind the overly technical approach, which really did not suit his flamboyant all guns blazing style of play. And I believe if Seve had the information contained in this book, he would have understood more about getting in and staying in the 'zone'. This would have helped him to control his emotions more and then we would have seen even more amazing and wonderful golf from him, which could easily have resulted in many more Major wins befitting his immense talent.

And this applies to other golfers who have an instinctive natural approach to the game, don't get bogged down by focussing on the technicalities of the game; you can do all of this when you are on the practice course. When you go out to play, enjoy and express yourself with passion and excitement, fully embrace these energies because this is how you access the higher vibrations and this is how you love to play the game. This is when you will also play your best golf.

I expect many professionals around the world can identify with this, when they were young, carefree and just loved to play, before life's responsibilities came along and it all got too serious. I am sure for many of them this is when they probably played some of the most exciting and finest golf of their lives. And the one's that went on to great careers maybe it wasn't because they were the best, maybe they had a little less inner resistance getting in the way when it mattered or just bought into the inevitable negativity when it came along a little less that the rest.

Dr Rotella goes on to talk about Brad Faxon who at one point in his career had fearful thoughts about using his driver. These thoughts even occurred not only when teeing off but also at other impromptu moments, even during his sleep. This made him unsure about using his driver and for some time he used his three wood instead.

I see this as his inner resistance going to work on him to get what it wanted, negative energy. It seized the opportunity and developed a negative thinking and feeling pattern around his driver. This was great for his inner resistance plenty of emotional negativity to recharge its batteries but a nightmare for Brad. I would have explained to Brad what was happening and got him to focus on watching his thoughts in order to stop his inner resistance from using this method to recharge itself at his expense.

The Notebook in the first Module would have been perfect for Brad to follow; this would have stopped the momentum of his negative thoughts and feelings, which would have then weakened his inner resistance in respect of using his driver. The result would be less feelings of fear around his driver allowing him to stay in the higher vibrations when standing on the tee; this would have then allowed him to get back to feeling comfortable using it. He could also have followed one of the other modules to focus his conscious mind on a good feeling place when playing the shot rather than let it be open to being infected with negative thoughts from his inner resistance. This would have helped rebuild his confidence and belief back up around that club.

This can happen with any aspect of your game, putting, short game, irons etc. Your inner resistance can capitalise on any worries or doubts blowing them out of all proportion, the next thing you know you are struggling with something that you used to feel complete confidence with.

You have fallen into a negative thinking pattern about a certain part of your game due to your inner resistance. You can still play the shot as well as you always could but now when you pick up that club this triggers off your inner resistance and you are flooded with fear and doubts. Gaining control of your inner resistance here is the key.

It's your inner resistance that you are tussling with not your ability to hit a golf shot and the negative thoughts that it is pushing into your mind is what is sapping your confidence.

One great piece of advice that Dr Rotella gives is *'No matter what happens with any shot you hit, accept it. Acceptance is the last step in a sound routine'*. From a HVT viewpoint acceptance is **absolutely essential**, as 'non acceptance' means you have emotionally bought into the bad shot and allowed negativity in, again dragging you down in vibration into a more negative place. The result being you are then far more likely to make more mistakes and mess up. The answer of course is keep your vibration up so don't buy into anything negative your focus must be as always inner peace and serenity.

I consider acceptance of your previous shot or shots as one of the most important disciplines to master and many golfers do not pay heed to this and constantly suffer the consequences. Hopefully now, thanks to HVT showing us exactly why acceptance is so important more golfers will make the effort to follow this practice.

Another great piece of advice about putting Dr Rotella gives is *'A good putting attitude is free of fear. The golfer has to believe the putt will go in the hole, but he must not care if he misses'*.

So true and from a HVT perspective allowing fear in means a drop in vibration and worrying about whether the ball goes in the hole or not simply allows negative energy in by the back door and the result is the same, a drop in vibration. You must always putt from inner peace and serenity and with no attachment whatsoever to the outcome. If you sink it great, if you miss it doesn't affect your inner peace and serenity one bit, this keeps your vibration at the highest possible level and this means you are in the best possible mindset for the next shot.

If you care if it misses before your putt then this means you are anticipating this potentially happening and allowing in subtle waves of anxiety therefore increasing the chances that it might. You must shut this door and really have no emotions about it maybe missing, just as you must feel no disappointment if it does.

This keeps you in the 'high zone' or as near to it as possible. Even when you are playing in the 'high zone' you will still have the odd shot that doesn't go to plan, so be ever vigilant and never ever allow negativity to grip your mind, it will always be waiting in the wings for an opportune moment.

As you can see mind management is essential to keep you at as high a vibration as possible thus holding your form. Your inner resistance is the enemy and you must keep it quiet if you want to produce your best form more consistently.

HVT brings a new perspective and allows us to look at how we control our mind on the golf course in a new and empowering way; this offers simple solutions that can be incorporated into your game to ensure you are always in as high a vibration as possible.

Constantly being aware of your vibration is the key, this allows you through the various modules to tinker with it always looking to attain the best mindset at any given time. This is how you stay in or as close to the high zone as possible.

Chapter 20

The Yips, Shanking and other problems

Many golfers suffer from the 'Yips' and shanking, either of which can be extremely disheartening when they strike. The 'Yips' is a muscle twitch just as you are playing the shot and shanking is when you hit the ball off the heel and it squirts to the side. The problem is once you are afflicted with these annoying niggles it can sometimes be difficult to stop them happening.

I will have a look at both of the problems through HVT eyes to see if I can shed a new light on them and come up with a new way of dealing with them.

The Yips

The dreaded 'Yips' can affect anybody and usually it is when putting although it can be evident in other shots such as chipping or even driving. It is an involuntary twitch, a muscle jerk just as you play the shot and many great players have suffered from this, it has even ended careers.

Three possible causes have been identified:

1. Performance Anxiety:

This can be caused by over thinking such as being too aware of the technicalities of your swing, excessive analysing of the shot or even worrying what people are thinking of you all of which can create anxiety. How do I look? What if I mess up? Is my swing okay? Etc, and this type of fear based self-conscious thinking opens the door for your inner resistance to flood you with doubts, resulting in anxious feelings in other words negative energy, which creates a drop in your vibration and as a result the dreaded 'Yips'.

2. S.E.E. Significant Emotional Event:

This occurs when you have a very negative experience such as you are leading your home club competition by five shots with five holes to play, your family and friends are watching and you hit your drive into the pond letting it all slip away and missing out on winning the tournament, a tournament that you always had your heart set on. This could plunge you down the vibrations and into a negative depressed state of mind.

Severe negative experiences like this, which could be compared to a mild trauma cut so deep and are such a rapid drop in vibration that they leave a residue of powerful negative energy which along with other similar experiences collect over time forming a strong negative presence within you and it is this slow vibrating trapped negative energy that may be causing you to have the 'Yips'.

This negative presence or residue is what I refer to as your inner resistance which in this case may be caused by severe negative golf experiences. Although that is not to say other major negative experiences outside of golf such as divorce, health issues, bereavement, job loss, childhood issues etc could not also contribute to the negative energy presence that has collected within you resulting in the manifestation of the 'Yips'.

3. Focal Dystonia:

This is a neurological dysfunction affecting specific muscles; misfiring neurons in the brain are thought to be the cause. And some research even suggests that practising your putting makes it worse as it carves the dysfunctional neuron pathways in the brain even deeper. This is borne out by the fact that some golfers find the more they practice the worse the 'Yips' get.

What can you do?

Looking at the three recognised causes leads me to the conclusion that two of them 'Performance Anxiety' and 'S.E.E'. are certainly inner resistance (mind) related and the third 'Focal Dystonia' even though it appears that it is not mind related could lead to issues in this area by creating within you the fear or nervous apprehension of the Yips potentially happening. So it is advisable to follow some of the modules in this book to release and manage your inner resistance in order to raise your vibration for all three causes.

Work at getting rid of your inner resistance by using modules one, two or three and you will be helping release the negative emotional energy that is trapped within you, which may be causing the problem. Module two 'Energy Diffusing' may be particularly useful as you can focus this on the specific negative energy ball that relates to the 'Yips'.

Also using any of the other modules such as the 'inner lake' will help when you are playing your shot by taking your conscious mind to one side and concentrating it on serenity and inner peace, this will ease your anxious feelings therefore alleviating the potential of the 'Yips' occurring if performance anxiety is the problem. Keep practicing these techniques and it should certainly help.

If you are suffering from the neurological problem 'Focal Dystonia' it appears the answers to this are more technical such as becoming more dominant with the hand that is not experiencing the 'Yips' and using the 'Yips' affected hand in a less involved way. So if your right hand is the affected hand grip the club essentially with the left hand and gently rest the right hand on top for stability. Or even putt left handed if you are normally right handed and vice versa.

Anything that in a sense recruits a new set of neurons to complete the action of playing the shot may be the cure as this takes you away from the old neuron route with the fault.

If it is a neurological issue I still advise using the modules to help as well because the higher up you can get your vibration the less affected you should be by the 'Yips'.

My plan for dealing with the 'Yips' whatever the cause would be:

1. Use modules one, two and three to break down and release your inner resistance.
2. Use module seven 'inner lake' when taking your shot to hold you in a more positive less anxious mindset.
3. Train yourself not to react and hold onto your serenity when you do experience the 'Yips' and this will help you by not adding to your inner resistance. If you emotionally buy into it you are recharging your inner resistance and solidifying the problem increasing the chances of it happening again.
4. After practicing this for a while if it is still not cured it is probably a neurological issue so look at a new grip or putting other way round this is something your club professional should be able to advise you on.

Shanking

This is when the golfer hits the ball off the heel or hosel of the club and it squirts off to the side. This may be caused by poor technique and if this is the case your club professional will be able to deal with this but again this can lead to mind related issues, a drop in confidence, developing a fear of shanking, tension etc.

To deal with the mind related side of things getting your conscious mind out of the way when you play the shot will be a great help. Tension in your arms and hands is thought to be the main reason for people shanking the ball when it is a mind related issue and this is generally created by indecision and fear in other words 'performance anxiety'.

So use a module that gets you concentrating on serenity and inner peace while you take the shot with a sense of non-detachment to the outcome of the actual shot this will help keep anxiety out of your mind. It does not affect your inner peace if you hit a good shot or squirt one off to the side either way you hold your inner peace.

Training yourself not to react emotionally when a shank happens if it is a mind related problem will help because the emotional reaction is what your inner resistance is after. Don't give it this negative emotional energy and it will soon cease prompting the thoughts into your mind that you may shank it because it is not working for it, it is not getting the negative feelings from you that it needs therefore curing the problem. This also applies to the 'Yips'.

Also concentrating on a high vibrational mindset (serenity and inner peace) will relax you and take any tension out of your body giving you a positive focal point releasing any indecision and fear. Taking three deep breaths before your shot will help you to relax.

Quick fix tips for the Yips and Shanking

I advise the following quick fix routine for either the Yips or shanking as you are playing your shot:

1. Three deep breaths (to relax and release tension).
2. Use module 7. the inner lake (this will help take your conscious mind out of play alleviating anxiety).
3. If you do 'Yip' or shank it no negative reaction.

This little routine will help train you to counteract negativity coming from within your own mind and settle you down for the shot holding you in the best possible vibrational place. Also give it time to work as you will have to educate your inner resistance that you are no longer going to give it what it wants when you make either of these errors.

It's like when you get bullied the bully gets nothing from the interaction if you do not emotionally react. If you don't allow yourself to 'feel' hurt the bully gets no boost up of superiority, power etc and will soon stop bothering you. In fact if you master non-reaction the bully actually feels depleted or dragged down in vibration when they fail to get a reaction out of you, it's the same for your inner resistance it will soon stop if you don't react because it's getting nothing, it is in fact losing energy.

Non-reaction puts you in charge and takes the power away from your inner resistance keeping you in as high a vibration as possible and every time you manage to do it, it also releases some of your inner resistance therefore weakening it in the process. This raises your vibration and this is why practising and mastering this discipline is so important and it is also something you can practice in your everyday life outside of golf.

Other problems

It's also worth mentioning that whether you have experienced a 'S.E.E'. (Significant Emotional Event) relating to golf or not, you still have inner resistance and this negative residue is what is triggering your 'Performance Anxiety' attacks. And when this happens it may lead to issues other than the Yips or shanking because you are dragged down into a more negative zone. Your arms, hands and body may tense up and this can make it very difficult to play your normal game. This can mean lots of things going wrong such as topped shots, miss hit shots, hooks, slices and even fresh air shots etc. And when this grips hold of you things can quickly go downhill as you feel yourself sinking into a very negative state.

The anxiety can just come over you possibly due to being tired or even thinking about something outside of golf that has been bothering you. Or it can be brought on by playing with a different group to your usual pals, a competition, money at stake in a bet, in contention on the back nine, an important shot, anything that adds a touch of pressure often triggers it and that's all your inner resistance needs to spark into life and begin flooding you with negative thoughts.

The best course of action is to follow the 'quick tips fix' to settle the energies down when you play each shot and this will help get your conscious mind out of the way. It's your conscious mind that is seeping in anxiety so get it thinking about something else that focuses it on serenity, inner peace, fun, joy etc and this should settle things down and get your vibration back up.

You could also before your game use module 4 the driftwood meditation to get yourself in the best possible serene mindset when you think it may flare up. It's always a good idea to do what you can to set your vibration before you play at the highest possible level.

I have seen players lose form and be struggling then suddenly change their mood somehow, maybe by making a joke of something and this can change the whole energy dynamics. The mood switch has been flicked by engaging the wonderful high energy of laughing and the next thing they are feeling different and this is the key to jumping up in vibration and instantly rediscovering their form. Humour is a powerful tool to change your vibration from slow to fast and get yourself back on track.

When a player is having a hard time and struggling often you can hear comments like he has lost concentration and needs to up the intensity. This means when a player has really fallen down the vibrations and his mind is scattered and under attack from his inner resistance, by concentrating on what he is doing with great intensity he can get his focus off the negativity that is swarming all over him.

This will help lift him back up in vibration (as he disengages the negativity) and facilitate some improvement in his form, and then from there he will be better placed to hopefully move towards higher vibrational thoughts and feelings and get himself going in the right direction vibrationally speaking.

Many golfers slip into a determined intense mode when it really matters such as in contention in the final holes, this helps keep their inner resistance under control when it may well flare up and they can still play pretty good golf from this mindset but it's nothing compared to the golf they are capable of playing in the high zone.

Remember if you have lost form you are down in vibration and that means negativity is seeping in somewhere so look to get yourself back up the vibrations by changing your mood and heading back towards serenity and inner peace. Laughing, joking, thinking of something that gives you good feelings, positive visualising, focussing on happy times etc can all help to change your mood and get the ball rolling.

You can snap out of a slump by practicing these techniques just try them all and see what suits you. Find your favourites and use them when the time arises. The piece of driftwood I talked about to use as a physical trigger is really powerful, so think about other physical triggers that may suit you that you could carry to the same effect. It could be a photograph of your children or partner, or even a place that brings back happy memories, or a lucky charm that you believe in, or a cherished item that was given to you by somebody very important in your life, which creates good feelings within you.

Whatever it is the idea is that by holding it in your hand for a moment or just touching it, or even thinking about it changes what you are feeling. It would be something that generates positive happy memories, good feelings so you can tap into this energy and if you practice this it will become second nature and it's a great way to flick the switch and change your mood.

Its straight forward, better mood means higher vibration, means better golf.

Do you deserve success?

Lots of players are held back by what they believe they deserve but what does that really mean? Well this is related to your self-esteem, your opinion of yourself, so if you don't have a healthy positive opinion of yourself then you may struggle to close the victory when you have the chance, you may just miss out on the big win when you have the opportunity, in fact success may elude you in lots of different ways not just on the golf course.

This can happen by becoming anxious and doubting yourself when it really matters and your form suffers, you may lose motivation, even feel ill, whatever way it manifests you just seem to find a way to let it slip away when the opportunity is there and many promising careers have been lost due to this. You have the knack of finding a way to fail, reasons why it's not going to work may pop up in your mind and you end up believing them. This pulls you down in vibration just far enough so you don't succeed.

If you do have a not too healthy opinion of yourself, it is generally because of the amount of love you received in the first six years of your life from your parents. If you didn't get much love during this time period or even if there was just a lot of negative energy around then this opens the door for your inner resistance to get a serious hold over you during your most sensitive and fragile years and form a stronger than usual negative presence.

Then in later years you have a lot of inner resistance, a lot battling against you especially when you are in line for success of some sort, this is when it really becomes active and works against you. This is because you have been living your life at a certain vibrational level (due to the inner resistance) and to have success means you would rise in vibration and your inner resistance doesn't want this, it wants to hold you back. It wants to keep you in the vibrational comfort zone it is used to.

It's not that you don't believe you deserve success, of course you do but in your case you have a little more negativity within you telling you that you don't. It is trying to hold you down where it feels more comfortable. If you had less inner resistance it wouldn't be such a loud strong negative voice within, it would be quieter and easier to ignore.

Work at getting rid of it and you will soon overcome this problem and then you will be somebody who finds that success comes a lot easier. Nearly every one of us is affected by this to some degree.

Answers to the three key questions:

1. What is the 'zone'?

The 'high zone' is a high vibrational place where negative energy does not exist.

2. How do you get there?

You train your conscious mind to embody high vibrational thoughts and more importantly **feelings**, such as serenity and inner peace, while at the same time allowing any negative thoughts and feelings that bubble up to gently fall away without engaging them. This allows you to rise in vibration into the 'high zone'.

3. Why can you play so well when you are there?

You can play so well because you are in the higher more refined vibrations, which are virtually free from negative energy so there is much less to infect and damage your game. And when you are here your conscious mind because it is freed up from your inner resistance naturally becomes immersed in and occupied by the good feelings and this maintains your vibration. This allows your all powerful subconscious mind also unhindered by your inner resistance because of the high vibration you are in to take over and play the shot and this is when the magic happens.

To summarise

The high zone is that magical place where you get the luck of the bounce, the run of the green and the help of the golfing gods, everything seems to go your way and you can't put a foot wrong. It's that day when you are playing golf at an altogether higher level and you make shots that are incredible and astounding even to yourself.

You feel at peace, serene, happy and totally in the flow as if you are somehow in harmony with everything around you. It almost feels like you are not even trying because it is all just happening for you while you bask in blissful serenity.

This magic can visit anybody and most golfers will have experienced it at sometime during their lives and been left wondering what on earth happened to them on that amazing day. Putts rolled in from all sorts of impossible lines, drives flew straight and true like never before and iron shots felt pure and sweet.

It is a place you go to, a vibration you ascend to by learning how to control your conscious mind and rise above your inner negativity (inner resistance) and at the same time you fall into a state of complete acceptance of 'what is'. This means you accept what comes your way without the usual instinctive negative reactions that automatically occur. You do not engage any potential negatives you just allow them to drift on by; it's all about controlling your emotions.

On this day you have no resistance to life's unfolding events, you are in a complete state of surrender to whatever happens. You feel slightly detached from your surroundings and you feel a sublime sense of inner peace, this state of mind raises your vibration and then your subconscious mind takes over the golf.

Tiger Woods has said *'my body just takes over and I get out of my own way'* a classic explanation of how it feels when your subconscious mind takes over.

Dr Gregg Steinberg Sports Psychologist to the PGA describes it in the following way:

'The zone, also known as flow, is that magical time on the course when we have complete confidence in our game, the hole gets in the way of every putt, and we can do no wrong. It is a time when this very difficult game seems so easy.

More importantly, the zone state is unique. More specifically, your feelings when in the zone state are unique. Sam Snead described the zone as a feeling of being "cool mad." When I am playing my best golf, I would describe it as a peaceful feeling'.

Understanding is the key, knowing exactly how it works and this is something that has largely eluded us until now but with the new insights high vibrational thinking brings we can now see clearly what the high zone is and how to get ourselves in it. It has never being clearer.

This will open the flood gates for golfers across the world to be able to train themselves to attain the high zone at will. Follow the mind training techniques in this book and you will soon be playing the golf of your life.

Raise your vibration!

Get into the 'High Zone'

Play the greatest golf of your life!

HVT Consultancy

For the very latest in Golf Psychology
The most powerful methods available today to get you in the
'High Zone'

One to one consultation
Strategy assessment for mind management based on personal
needs
HVT implementation plan
High Vibrational Mind Therapy

Contact

Steve Wharton
Author and founder of High Vibrational Mind Therapy
www.hvt-consultancy.com

Printed in Great Britain
by Amazon